Rufus Jones and the Presence of God

Rufus Jones and the Presence of God

Helen Holt

CHRISTIAN ALTERNATIVE
BOOKS

Winchester, UK
Washington, USA

JOHN HUNT PUBLISHING

First published by Christian Alternative Books, 2023
Christian Alternative Books is an imprint of John Hunt Publishing Ltd.,
No. 3 East St., Alresford, Hampshire SO24 9EE, UK
office@jhpbooks.com
www.johnhuntpublishing.com
www.christian-alternative.com

For distributor details and how to order please visit the 'Ordering' section on our website.

Text copyright: Helen Holt 2022

ISBN: 978 1 80341 342 6
978 1 80341 343 3 (ebook)
Library of Congress Control Number: 2022947005

A CIP catalogue record for this book is available from the British Library.

Design: Lapiz Digital Services

UK: Printed and bound by CPI Group (UK) Ltd, Croydon, CR0 4YY
Printed in North America by CPI GPS partners

We operate a distinctive and ethical publishing philosophy in
all areas of our business, from our global network of authors to
production and worldwide distribution.

Contents

Author of *Quakers and Science* (Christian Alternative Books, 2023). ISBN 978-1-80341-139-2
Mysticism and the Inner Light in the Thought of Rufus Jones, Quaker (Brill, 2022). ISSN 1566-208X

For my siblings, Richard and Sonia

Preface

How are human beings related to God? Can experience, science or philosophy shed any light on the matter? What are the implications of such a relationship, if it exists? These are the questions that the American Quaker Rufus Jones wrestled with in the first half of the twentieth century. He concluded that humans and God were in fact intimately related, and discussed his ideas in terms of the Inner Light and mysticism. The Inner Light was a way of expressing his belief that God is present within us, as part of our very nature. Mysticism was a way of exploring his conviction that all of us can know this presence.

Born in 1863, Jones has been described as a Quaker giant of the twentieth century, in large part because he is widely credited with revitalizing significant swathes of the Religious Society of Friends by casting Quakerism as a mystical religion that was consistent with the latest discoveries in psychology. He sought to share his vision through numerous books, and was much in demand as a speaker, both in his native America and further afield. His mission to popularize mysticism was made that much more interesting, however, because he was active at a particularly tumultuous time in the history of Quakerism, when Quakers were attempting to come to terms with the advances in science and biblical criticism that were challenging old formulations of faith. Thus, while some wholeheartedly embraced Jones' ideas, relieved that he had made faith and their experience of God intellectually credible, others were dismayed or even outraged, accusing him of taking Christ out of Quakerism and making the soul divine.

Controversies aside, as a person Jones was undoubtedly charismatic and is frequently described in glowing terms. The English Quaker John Hoyland, for example, enthused that, 'To a whole generation of us he was a prophet and a saint and a shining light. We loved him and we venerated him. He was the leader of our lives.'[1] The American pastor and radio-broadcaster Harry Emerson Fosdick wrote that he was 'natural, genuine, direct, human ... He possessed the spiritual vitality he pled for, and he shared it'.[2] And his biographer David Hinshaw proclaimed that there was something Olympian about him, in that those who knew him felt instinctively that his faith would enable him to meet any crisis in life.

Today, we might describe Jones as 'authentic' or 'integrated': his spiritual convictions matched his actions, and he saw no contradiction between his religious beliefs and the latest developments in philosophy and science. We might also describe him as someone who was spiritually creative, in that he developed novel ways of looking at important spiritual concepts and inspired others with his spiritual vision and vitality. Although the science and philosophy of the early twentieth century are different in many ways from today's, there is, I think, still a lot we can learn from Jones, both about his conviction that faith should take the latest knowledge onboard and about the everyday spiritual practices that made him the man he was.

Fortunately, there is an abundance of material to draw on to gain some insight into Jones' life and thought.[3] He wrote hundreds of editorials for Quaker journals and over 50 books – all for the general public rather than academics. The books include historical studies of mysticism, advice about the spiritual life, and children's stories based on the Bible. Especially interesting are half a dozen autobiographical works, some of which give charming accounts of his childhood in rural Maine. Reminiscent of Huckleberry Finn for their tales of adventures and misadventures, they are shot through with spiritual reflections and give us an insight into the convictions and experiences that shaped Jones' future life and beliefs. There is also a fascinating collection of archived letters both to and from Jones at Haverford College, where he taught for most of his career. The personal content of these letters, expressed in cramped or flamboyant cursive script, provides a glimpse of some of the emotions that were accompanying theological upheavals. Some of them are reproduced in the following pages.

In this short book, we'll look first at the life of Rufus Jones, tracing his journey from farm-boy to influential Quaker leader and reformer. We'll then explore how he came to hold the views that he did, discovering how he sought to integrate insights from people as varied as his prophetic and saintly Aunt Peace, the second-century theologian Clement of Alexandria, and the so-called father of modern psychology, William James. With this foundation in place, we'll be in a position to understand why Jones believed what he did, assess whether his arguments are convincing, and appreciate why his ideas about the relationship between God and humans delighted some and worried others. Finally, we'll identify some of the spiritual practices that might have contributed to Jones' spiritual maturity and to his ability, in the phrase associated with the seventeenth-century Brother Lawrence, to practise the presence of God.

Acknowledgements

I am grateful to Rex Ambler for his insightful comments on an earlier version of this book, to Sarah Horowitz at Haverford College library for scanning letters from the Rufus Jones Special Collection for me, and to Anna Zoe Hodge for proofreading the manuscript.

1

A small-town boy: Introducing Rufus Jones

In later life, Jones would rub shoulders with leading academics, visit Gandhi at his Ashram, and exchange many letters about war-related relief work with the future president Herbert Hoover. All of these relationships bear the stamp of his Quaker upbringing. Jones was born on 25 January, 1863, into an extended Quaker family in rural South China, Maine. His mother, Mary Hoxie Jones, and father, Edwin Jones, both came from long lines of Quakers and already had two children – Alice, then four, and Walter, ten (Herbert was born four years later). The family lived in a farmhouse, which they shared with Edwin's mother, Susannah, and his unmarried sister, Peace. Susannah was an immensely capable, pipe-smoking Quaker elder who embodied the pioneer spirit. She had had eleven children, nine of whom survived, and enthralled the young Jones with tales of 'Indians' and lakes so thick with herrings that you could walk on their backs. Jones described Peace as a refined and saintly woman with remarkable spiritual gifts and a unique understanding of him. She was to have a lasting and profound spiritual impact on his life, and when she held the newborn Jones in her arms she calmly (and, as it turns out, accurately) announced that, 'This child will one day bear the message of the Gospel to distant lands and to peoples across the sea.'[1]

In his autobiographies, Jones tells of how every day before breakfast, even though there was work to be done on the farm, there was a long period of silent family worship during which all the older members seemed to be plainly communing in joyous fellowship with a real Presence, with the little folk caught up into the experience and carried along with the others. 'We went to work, or we went to school, out of a living, throbbing hush of silence in which something more than form or formal prayer had taken place,' he wrote, concluding that, 'Here it was that I learned the nearness and the reality of God as spiritual operating presence.'[2] By age four he was joining the two-hour mostly silent Quaker meeting for worship, where he says the silence came over him as a kind of spell with a life of its own and he found a gleam of eternal reality breaking through. This sense of the presence of God as an everyday experience was so natural that he claimed that as a child he had no more difficulty in seeing Jacob's ladders going from earth to heaven than he did in seeing where the best apples grew.

There were also family Bible readings every morning and evening, and Jones began to go to Bible School when he was six. The Bible took on a particularly intense role in his life when, at age ten, he entered what he called one of the great crises of his life. A seemingly innocent bruise on his foot was lanced by a well-intentioned but woefully uninformed doctor who had sharpened his knife on a scythe stone in the family barn. Not surprisingly, Jones' foot and leg became badly infected, and he was bedbound in considerable pain for nine months. After some discussion, it was decided that he would spend his days by reading the Bible out loud to his grandmother as she knitted. After struggling with the unpronounceable names in the 'begat' chapters, he was caught up in the story of Abraham and recalls that he finished reading about Joseph with tears running down his face. Jones had recuperated by the time he got to the New Testament, but felt that the Old Testament was the book of his boyhood, enthusing that, 'It gave me my first poetry and my first history, and I got my growing ideas of God from it.'[3] In later years he would be grateful for the fact that although his family was not familiar with the rise of biblical criticism taking place in universities, they followed George Fox in believing that the Bible was inspired but not God's final word. This, he said, allowed him to embrace both science and biblical teaching, enabling him to find and love the Bible's treasures while making use of all that science and history had revealed.

In spite of this religious milieu, Jones could certainly not be described as pious, and in *A Small-Town Boy* he reflects on how life in a rural community shaped his character. He would often leave the house early to avoid being given chores, he admitted, preferring to have fun with his friends. As the unofficial leader of the local farm-boys, he cultivated a spirit of daring and courage through physical challenges – climbing on 'perilous roofs', diving fully clothed and booted into rivers to prepare for a possible capsize in a canoe, and, literally, skating on thin ice (not always successfully). He also tells of drinking a barrel of cider that a farmer had carelessly left lying around, and, on one memorable occasion, skipping school to sneak into a house that was being hauled along the frozen lake by oxen to a new location, thoroughly enjoying the view from the second floor of this 'mighty palanquin'. His oratorical skills were honed at the local grocery store, where the owner had Jones mount the counter to read important newspaper articles to the men sitting on chairs and barrel heads and boxes. 'It was here on the counter,' wrote Jones, 'that I first learned how to articulate clearly and to get ideas across effectively to a body of listeners.'[4] He was also deeply affected by the wild beauty of Maine, reminiscing about the bald eagles that nested near the lake (glorious birds with a wing-stretch of over seven feet that were older than the Constitution of the United States and as completely dedicated to freedom), the distant mountains, and the occasional ecstatic cry of loons that revealed their complete unity with creation. There were also twice-weekly rides to Quaker meetings through majestic forests – in winter, as the cart creaked through the snow, the young Jones would sit near a hot soapstone under a buffalo robe. This appreciation of natural beauty, he concluded, kept him morally and spiritually safe.

Jones studied at a local Quaker school, and then boarded at the Quaker Oak Grove Seminary in Vassalboro (Maine) in 1878/79. During the summer of 1879, while hoeing potatoes, he told his father that he wanted to continue his education. Surprised, his father (whom Jones once described as 'not a thinker') asked, 'Why, thee's got all the education thee needs?', but told Jones he was free to go if his mind was made up. It was, and shortly afterwards he was awarded a scholarship to study at the Friends School in Providence, Rhode Island. Following his graduation in 1881 he stayed on for a further year to meet college requirements, and in 1882 enrolled at Haverford College, a small but respected Quaker college just outside Philadelphia, where he studied history, philosophy and religion.

After graduating from Haverford, Jones spent a year travelling in Europe. He returned to America in 1887 to teach at Providence Friends School, and the following year married a fellow Quaker, Sarah (known as Sallie) Coutant. From 1889 to 1893 he was Principal of Oak Grove Seminary, where Sallie taught botany and acted as matron. One of her former pupils described her as an outstanding beauty and very capable, and some of her letters reveal a dry sense of humour. In 1892 the couple had a son, whom they named Lowell after Jones' favourite poet. Jones was immediately besotted, counting Lowell's birth as one of the supreme events of his life and one that filled their home with an unutterable emotion of joy and wonder.

Jones returned to his alma mater, Haverford College, in 1893, where he taught psychology, philosophy and Christian history for the rest of his career. He loved the job, reflecting that, 'I have always felt that I was at my best in a classroom, and there is no question that I am happiest when I am teaching a class of youth.'[5] He remained a prominent figure on campus well after his retirement, and today the College's Rufus Jones Society seeks to promote leadership informed by the principles and example of Jones' life and work.

The first decade at Haverford, however, saw many highs and lows in Jones' personal life. Sallie contracted tuberculosis and, in spite of lengthy treatment in the Adirondacks, died in 1899. In 1902 he married Elizabeth Bartram Cadbury, an intelligent, reserved woman who was very active on Quaker committees and whose proficiency in German would prove to be an immense help to Jones in his study of German mystics. Tragedy was to strike again in 1903 though, when the 11-year-old Lowell died from diphtheria, a loss made all the harder because Jones was en route to England at the time, having believed Lowell to be over the worst of the illness. In 1904, Jones and Elizabeth had a baby girl, Mary. As an adult she was heavily involved in Quaker work and acted as her father's secretary between 1929 and 1934. Jones' own father died in a railroad accident in 1904, and in 1905 his close friend and fellow reformer John Wilhelm Rowntree died shortly after arriving in America to see him. Just a year before, Jones had written a heartfelt dedication to Rowntree in one of his books: a 'Dear friend over the sea with whom I have had a new revelation of the riches of human fellowship and the still deeper joy of fellowship with our Divine Companion'.[6] Figure 1 is a letter from Jones to Rowntree, joyfully reporting the birth of Mary and seeking permission for the proposed dedication.

Alongside his teaching career, Jones churned out books on mysticism, the spiritual life, and the history of Quakerism at the rate of one or two a year. They were relatable, readable, and sprinkled with poetry and homely analogies, and Jones has been credited with making mysticism middlebrow, paving the way for the success of later books such as *The Seven Storey Mountain*, the 1948 autobiography of the Trappist monk Thomas Merton.

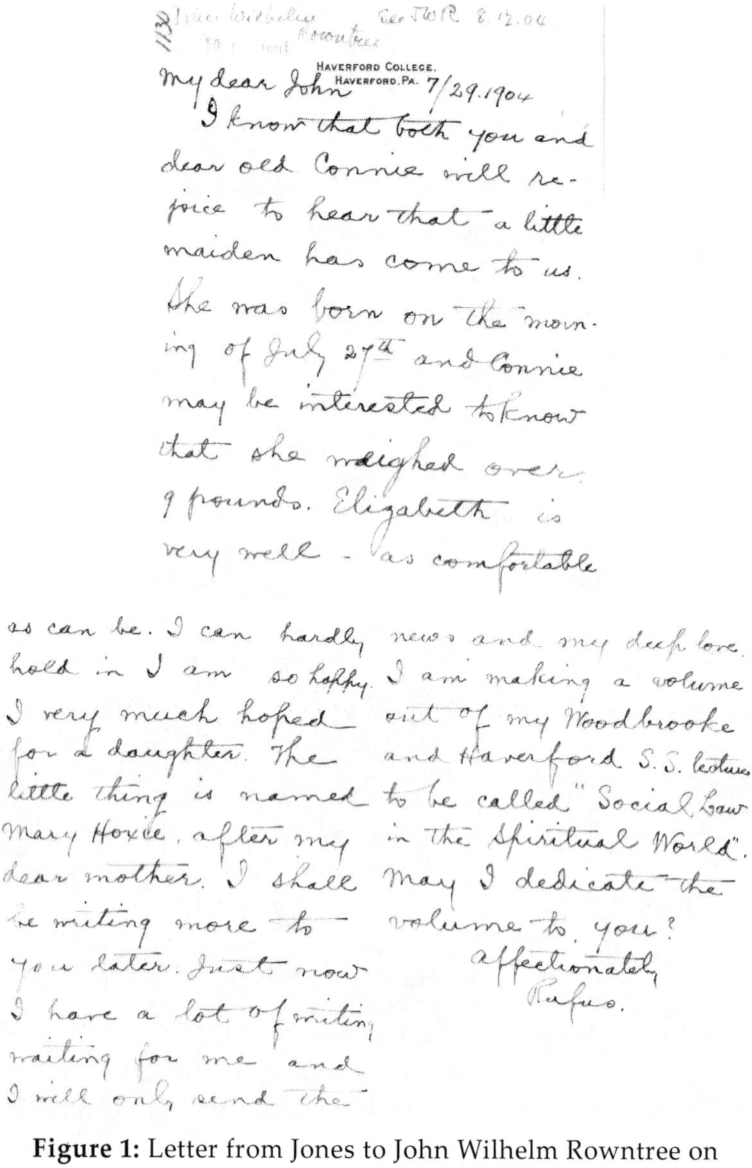

HAVERFORD COLLEGE.
HAVERFORD, PA. 7/29.1904

My dear John

I know that both you and dear old Connie will rejoice to hear that a little maiden has come to us. She was born on the morning of July 27th and Connie may be interested to know that she weighed over 9 pounds. Elizabeth is very well - as comfortable as can be. I can hardly hold in I am so happy. I very much hoped for a daughter. The little thing is named Mary Hoxie, after my dear mother. I shall be writing more to you later. Just now I have a lot of writing waiting for me and I will only send the news and my deep love. I am making a volume out of my Woodbrooke and Haverford S.S. lectures to be called "Social Law in the Spiritual World". May I dedicate the volume to you?

affectionately
Rufus.

Figure 1: Letter from Jones to John Wilhelm Rowntree on 29 July 1904 reporting the birth of Mary and asking for permission for the proposed dedication.[7]

He also took on a number of high-profile roles within Quakerism, including editing various Quaker journals. It was common practice for individuals to subscribe to a journal at the time, as they were an important means of sharing news and disseminating ideas, and each of the main strands of Quakerism had its own publication. It was a somewhat precarious time to be an editor, however, as fault-lines were emerging between evangelical Quakers, who favoured literal interpretations of the Bible, and liberal Quakers. The latter were keen to embrace the latest developments in science and the 'higher criticism' that was treating the Bible as divinely inspired but written by humans in a particular cultural context rather than as being the inerrant word of God. Jones' appointment at Haverford was linked to his taking on the role of editor of the liberal Quaker journal *The Friends Review*. The following year, partly in an attempt to heal breaches between different strands of Quakerism and partly for financial reasons, the decision was taken to merge the *Review* with the evangelical *The Christian Worker* to form *The American Friend*. Jones became editor of the merged publication, and as a consequence had to negotiate tensions between evangelical and liberal views. It was a difficult balance, and there are many letters in the Haverford archives from disgruntled readers. British Quakers (especially after the Manchester Conference of 1895) generally embraced the liberal agenda more readily than their American counterparts, and Jones received much-valued support from across the Atlantic. A ditty scrawled by Edward Grubb, editor of *The British Friend*, at the end of a letter to Jones sums up his difficulties: 'An American editor, Rufus, / Each Monday encountered a new fuss. / Correspondents, like bees, / Deprived him of ease, / But he cornered them all – good old Rufus!'[8]

Jones also attempted to create unity between these different strands of Quakerism through personal connections. He travelled widely across America to meet leading Quakers, clocking up an average of 10,000 miles a year for over a decade. In a pre-car era this was no mean feat, and the physical challenge was made much more difficult because Jones had an undiagnosed allergy to horses, meaning that journeys from train stations by horse and cart often left him breathless to the extent that it seemed as if each breath would be the last he could draw.

After America joined the First World War in 1917, Jones was instrumental in setting up the American Friends Service Committee (AFSC), an organization that he chaired on and off until 1944. In 1947 it was jointly awarded the Nobel Peace Prize with its British sister organization, the Friends Service Council. Just prior to retirement, he was also involved in the laymen's foreign mission, travelling widely in Asia, and, controversially at the time, advocating learning from other religions. Still active in his mid-70s, in 1938 he led a delegation of Quakers to Germany to plead the cause of the Jews to the Gestapo, braving a winter sea-crossing with a heavy cold. The meeting was ultimately unsuccessful, but, wonderfully incongruously, Jones and his three companions held an impromptu Quaker silent meeting for worship in the offices of the Gestapo while awaiting a response to their request: 'We bowed our heads,' recalled Jones, 'and entered upon a time of deep quiet meditation and prayer.'[9] Jones died in 1948 aged 85, in bed convalescing after a series of heart attacks. True to form, he had spent the morning working – correcting the proofs for his latest book and finishing a speech he was due to deliver a few days later.

It is probably clear, even from this brief sketch of his life, that Jones was impressively productive in multiple areas. He is perhaps best remembered, however, for his study and promotion of mysticism and for his associated ideas about that key Quaker concept, the Inner Light. The Inner Light can be viewed as a way to signify the presence of God within, and mysticism can be viewed as the experience of that presence. Jones began to interpret Quakerism as a mystical religion at college, and shortly after graduating, while considering his future career on a solitary Alpine walk, he had a religious experience in which he was overcome by a sense of God's presence and saw stretching before him 'an unfolding of labor in the realm of mystical religion'.[10] In the next chapter, we'll look in a bit more detail at the people who influenced Jones' view of mysticism, through their lives, their teaching, or their books.

2

Kindling flames: Inspiring people

'Nobody knows,' mused Jones in a sermon in 1932, 'how the kindling flame of life and power leaps from one life to another ... You listen to a hundred persons unmoved and unchanged: you hear a few quiet words from the man with the kindling torch and you suddenly discover what life means for you forevermore.'[1] During his childhood, Jones' Aunt Peace and Uncle Eli would prove to be long-lasting kindling flames. Jones says he had never known anyone of richer, purer or nobler qualities than Peace, and that she combined an uncanny moral intuition with grace and gentleness. As was the custom at the time, she made many religious journeys through America, bringing back presents and stories from the inconceivably distant states of Ohio and Iowa! But what really struck the young Jones, he said, was the way in which God took care of her and told her what to do and say in every place she went, just as God did in Bible stories. In other words, Peace exemplified a close and vibrant relationship with God, and it was one that the young Jones was determined to experience for himself. Eli Jones and his wife, Sybil, were respected Quaker missionaries and teachers – they had travelled widely and had set up Quaker schools in Palestine. Jones describes Eli as having superior intellectual powers, although he was largely self-educated. It was from watching Eli, he said, that he realized that the goodness of character he was seeking was not something miraculous that dropped into a soul out of the sky but rather was something formed within as a person faithfully did their set tasks and went to work with an enthusiastic passion to help make other people good. Together, then, Jones' aunt and uncle impressed on him the importance of both a relationship with God *and* human effort, a combination that will prove to be central to Jones' ideas about human nature, as we'll see in the next chapter.

After Jones left South China to study, he encountered new 'kindling flames', which fuelled rather than dampened his childhood faith. There were two particularly formative periods in his education. The first was his time at Haverford College in Philadelphia as an undergraduate. The second was a year of postgraduate study at Harvard when he was in his mid-thirties.

Jones was at Haverford at a time when the need to reconcile science and religion was pressing for many Christians. Thomas Huxley, widely known as 'Darwin's bulldog', was at the peak of his reputation, and the adjustment between Christianity and evolution had not yet been thought through. Jones clearly felt the problem keenly, writing that, 'It will be difficult, perhaps impossible, for my readers now living in peace in the lee of the dykes, to realize in any vivid way what it was like to be thrown into that open sea when the euroclydon was in full sweep.'[2] Early attempts at reconciliation had centred on William Paley's 1802 *Evidences of the Existence and Attributes of the Deity*, which attempted to prove the existence of God from the design apparent in nature, for example, in the human eye. Jones was not impressed, however, complaining that Paley was barren soil that provided no nourishment for the soul.

Relief came when one of his teachers, Pliny Chase, brought a new book to class, declaring it to be by a 'new prophet' in the age of science. The book was *Natural Law in the Spiritual World*. The prophet was the Scottish biologist Henry Drummond, who was undoubtedly a kindling flame. Drummond aimed to show that spiritual laws and natural laws were related, so he discussed natural phenomena ranging from parasites to the environment and drew spiritual analogies. Jones enthused that, while the book was imperfect, it came like water to shipwrecked men. Its long-lasting influence is apparent in the fact that two decades later Jones would write a book entitled *Social Law in the Spiritual World*. The title is clearly a play on Drummond's book, and Jones said in the Introduction that he aimed to do for psychology what Drummond had done for biology.

Jones also took inspiration from poets. Traditionally, Quakers had viewed the arts with some suspicion, but by the 1880s attitudes had softened. Haverford in Jones' era certainly embraced poetry, and its President, Thomas Chase, was well connected to prominent literary men. He invited the academic and politician James Bryce to lecture the students on Dante, and Matthew Arnold (who wrote poems such as 'Dover Beach' describing the demise of religion) captured the imagination of the students all the more strongly because Chase's invitation to him was overruled by more cautious Haverford managers. Jones enthused that Chase gave his students the *feel* of great literature by demonstrating how it should be read in meter, and he taught some students, including Jones, Italian so that they could read Dante in the original. Jones writes about being 'almost saturated' with the poems of James Russell Lowell and also absorbed Wordsworth, Tennyson, and the Quaker poet John Greenleaf Whittier.

What was it about these poets that kindled Jones' spirit and imagination? Perhaps the themes of the sublime, nature and the supernatural that are associated with Romanticism would have resonated with the mystical element of his disposition, and with his love of the untamed and beautiful countryside of South China. Whatever the attraction, Jones' excursions into poetry were intertwined with his developing belief system. He later reflected that all his reading fed into his religious life and that the passages he selected for memorization almost always ministered to his growing faith. In particular, he credited Wordsworth and Coleridge as interpreting the spiritual life of humans in fresh and transforming ways because they had discovered that humans are essentially spiritual beings, a position that was central to his own later thought about the relationship between God and humans.

An important step in turning these initial ideas about and experiences of God into a coherent system of thought was Jones' encounter with the concept of mysticism. In his sixties, Jones reflected that many features of his later life were determined by his decision to write a graduating thesis on this subject. Mysticism as an area of academic study was just beginning to emerge in the latter half of the nineteenth century, and two writers had a particularly strong influence on Jones. The first was Robert Vaughan, who wrote the seminal *Hours with the Mystics* in 1856. The book presents a somewhat meandering history of mysticism in the form of a conversation among three friends as they settle down to enjoy wine and walnuts in front of the fire on a windy November evening. The three of them discuss, with occasional digressions as they move to the drawing room or enjoy a summer picnic, how mysticism found expression among different nations and in different periods. *Hours* did much to catapult mysticism into academic respectability and to generate public fascination in the topic, and it certainly captivated Jones, who read and re-read the book at Haverford.

The second writer was Ralph Waldo Emerson. Born in 1803, Emerson studied at Harvard Divinity School before becoming junior minister at a Unitarian church in Boston. In 1832 his resignation was reluctantly accepted when the congregation decided that they disagreed with his view that Jesus did not intend communion to be administered forever. After some time travelling in Europe, where he met and embraced the ideas of Coleridge, Wordsworth and Carlyle (the very poets admired by Jones), Emerson returned to Concord, Massachusetts. There he gathered around him a group that would become known as the Transcendental Club, with members holding that divinity pervaded humanity and nature. Emerson earned his living as an essayist, poet and orator. His message and style were stirring

('Hitch your wagon to a star'; 'We live among surfaces, and the true art of life is to skate on them'), rather than drily intellectual. As the poet Walt Whitman put it, 'I was simmering, simmering, simmering. Emerson brought me to a boil.'[3]

Interestingly, Emerson was influenced by Quakerism, and in fact described himself as more of a Quaker than anything else, saying that he believed in the 'still small voice', with that voice being Christ within us. He refers to a number of books about Quakerism in his journals, and his final arguments for a break with the church drew heavily on Clarkson's *Portraiture of Quakerism* (1806). Furthermore, the list of the eight individuals whom Emerson identified as having 'ministered to his highest wants' included two Quakers – the apothecary and abolitionist Edward Stabler, and the Quaker elder Mary Rotch, who argued that the Light Within, not the Bible, was the final authority in religion. Both seemed to have impressed Emerson with their first-hand experience of God and provided the inspiration for his acclaimed essay 'Self-Reliance', in which he encourages his readers to learn to detect and trust that gleam of light that flashes across the mind from within.

Jones first encountered Emerson as a more or less accidental choice of philosopher, picked to fulfil the requirements for a philosophy course, but given that Emerson took his inspiration from the Romantic poets and Quakerism, and that he was a gifted writer who appealed to the heart as well as the head, there is little wonder that he would prove to be a kindling flame. Emerson associated the Inward Light of Quakerism with the religious experience and revelation apparent in other strands of religion, and it was this that instigated a dramatic shift in perception within Jones. George Fox, one of the main founders of Quakerism, was transformed from a 'provincial' to a 'cosmopolitan' figure, and Jones reports that he became conscious for the first time that the heart of Quakerism was mysticism, and that it was this that was the 'secret' of his early religious life. These ideas permeate all of Jones' writing: he was not exaggerating when he called them 'epoch-making'.

A further significant concept that Jones took from Emerson was that of the Oversoul. He expressed the impact of the idea in a letter to his future wife, Elizabeth, in 1902: 'Now why didn't thee tell me more about the "Oversoul"? ... It has had so much to do with my life and I wish thee had given me thy glimpse.'[4] The essence of the idea that Emerson conceptualized so succinctly and that Jones embraced so readily is that God and humans are related, and that, through this relationship, humans are related to one another.

One more kindling flame, whose influence is apparent in Jones' understanding of Christianity, is Clement of Alexandria. Jones refers to Clement as one of his most loved religious guides and published a selection of his writings in 1910. Clement was born *ca.* 150, probably in Athens, where he studied philosophy. During his subsequent travels he discovered Christianity, converted, and settled in Alexandria, the then intellectual centre of the Roman world. He became a teacher at the Catechetical School in about 180, and died between 211 and 215.

Jones was struck by Clement's attempts to present Christianity in a way that the educated Greek world found acceptable. It resonated with how twentieth-century liberals were trying to make their message relevant to their own generation. He also appreciated Clement's willingness to draw on non-Christian poets and philosophers: 'Homer and Isaiah, Heraclitus and St. John, alike bear witness in his pages to the presence of an immortal Divine Word,' Jones enthused, 'breathing through men and guiding the race.'[5] This no doubt resonated with Jones' belief that poetry was inspired by and revealed God.

Jones took two phrases from Clement that crop up frequently in his writings. One is the 'harmonized man', which expresses the transformation that someone undergoes as they begin to hear and obey God. Jones described it as a profound conception that expresses a state in which goodness, which initially requires effort to achieve, has become natural and habitual. The other is the phrase 'mutual and reciprocal correspondence', which describes the integral relationship between humans and God.

Jones clearly received a broad education at Haverford, one that encompassed poetry, science and mysticism. Significantly, all these academic fields, which might be separate today, were intertwined: Drummond showed him that science and religion belonged together, and he discovered for himself that poetry and religion did likewise. Furthermore, Vaughan introduced him to mysticism as an experience that occurred throughout history and in different cultures, and from Emerson he deduced that Quakerism was a mystical religion and took the concept of the Oversoul. Clement reached across the centuries to reinforce his conviction that religion should adapt to fit new knowledge, and gave him the concept of the harmonized man. Years later, Jones would give these ideas a more academic treatment, at Harvard University.

Jones had originally intended to go to Harvard to study philosophy in 1889, but instead accepted the post of Principal at Oak Grove Seminary. In 1893 the opportunity arose again, and again was deferred, this time to take up the position at Haverford. Circumstances were finally favourable in 1900/01, which proved to be an exceptionally stimulating period. Jones arrived in the wake of President Charles Eliot's ambitious programme of expansion, building, and academic restructuring, and during what has been termed the Golden Age of American Philosophy: William James and Josiah Royce were engaged in vigorous but amicable philosophical sparring over the nature of God, and Francis Peabody was breaking new ground by introducing social concerns into the study of theology. All three men would act as kindling flames for Jones.

William James (brother of the novelist Henry James) is often referred to as the father of modern psychology. He began his academic career at Harvard in 1872 in physiology and spent the rest of his career periodically shifting between the departments of philosophy and psychology. His first major work was the seminal two-volume *Principles of Psychology*. More than 12 years in gestation, and running to more than 1400 pages, *Principles* was published in 1890 and quickly became the leading text in America, influencing generations of psychologists. (It even makes a cameo appearance in John Steinbeck's novel *East of Eden*, when the impoverished farmer Samuel living in 1890s America reveals his extravagant purchase of *Principles* to his son, swearing him to secrecy for fear his wife would run him off the ranch if she found out.) *Principles* covers many aspects of psychology, from the transmission of nervous impulses to the formation of habit. James followed *Principles* with the classic *The Varieties of Religious Experience* (1902) on religious psychology, which uses numerous case studies to illustrate topics such as religion and neurology, the religion of healthy-mindedness and the 'sick soul', conversion, and mysticism. Jones came across *Principles* at a local library while teaching at Oak Grove, exclaiming in his autobiography that 'No man with my interests could ever forget an event like that!'[6]

Jones would hold James in exceptionally high regard for the rest of his life. He had a portrait of him in his study, and a few months before he died wrote in a rather shaky hand to his daughter that he was reading a wonderful book on the James family. He began to correspond with James before he went to Harvard, and the correspondence was evidently both affirming and invigorating: Jones reports that James had the 'heartiest sympathy' for his interest in mysticism and devotion to Quaker ideals. 'It was a characteristic of James to see "genius" in every young man who confided in him,' he wrote. 'When you saw how enthusiastic this great man was over your half-born mental child, you were assured that it must be a superlative offspring.'[7]

What would prove to be crucial for Jones was James' view that the visible world is part of a spiritual universe that gives it its significance, and that a person's higher part is continuous with a 'more' of the same quality that operates in this wider universe. (If you notice a similarity to Emerson's view of the Oversoul here, it might be partly because Emerson was a close friend of James' father, Henry James senior.) The best way to describe this 'more', James thought, was in terms of the subconscious self. Thus, he concluded that 'whatever it may be on its *farther* side, the "more" with which in religious experience we feel ourselves connected is on its *hither* side the subconscious continuation of our conscious life'.[8] James saw many possible interpretations of the 'farther side', including but not limited to Christianity. Furthermore, the 'more' did not have to be infinite or solitary. It might even, he speculated, be a larger and more godlike self.

Jones used James' textbooks to teach psychology at Haverford, but, more importantly, he believed that mysticism should be studied through psychology, and James was his primary source in this endeavour. Jones thus used material from *Principles* and *Varieties* to argue that God was an integral part of human nature, and that the subconscious was the meeting place: it was here, he speculated, that there may be 'some real shekinah where we may meet with that Divine Companion, that More of Life, in whom we live'.[9] The crucial difference from James, though, is that while James did not associate the 'more' with the Christian God, Jones did.

When Jones finally did arrange to study at Harvard, however, he must have been disappointed to find that James was absent in Europe preparing the Gifford lectures – a prestigious and ongoing series of lectures at Scottish universities established in 1887 to promote the study of natural theology. Jones settled on four courses covering ethics, philosophy and social psychology, and formed lasting friendships with Josiah Royce and Francis Peabody.

Jones described Royce as the oddest-looking man since Socrates, with an extraordinary mind and the moral passion of a great prophet, who rolled out his sentences as if there was an immense pressure behind them. He was the leading American proponent of a philosophical system known as absolute idealism. His thought is complex, but essentially he argued that all aspects of reality, including those we experience as contradictory, are unified in the thought of a single all-encompassing consciousness, often referred to as the Absolute. William James disagreed with him, complaining that his conception was too abstract and lacked practical consequences, and the two were known for their friendly sparring in what was termed the 'Battle of the Absolute' (see Figure 2). Royce also respected the insights of mysticism, and on a number of occasions Jones quotes Royce as saying that mystics are 'thoroughgoing empiricists', namely people who rely on and learn from experience. Jones audited Royce's course on metaphysics, working through his book *The World and the Individual* (1899–1900). After nearly 1000 pages, Royce provides a no-doubt welcome summary: 'The one lesson of our entire course has thus been the lesson of the unity of finite and infinite ... of the World and all its Individuals, of the One and the Many, of God and Man.'[10]

Figure 2: William James (left) and Josiah Royce in 1903: Shooting the breeze or perhaps battling over the Absolute.

Much of Royce's thought chimed with Jones' ideas about the relationship between humans and God, and he credited Royce with having a larger influence on his intellectual development than any other person. In particular, Royce's conviction that human consciousness is part of God's consciousness was key, because for Jones it proved that God and humans are in mutual and reciprocal correspondence, as Clement put it. Just as he used James to provide a psychological justification for his conviction that God and humans are related, he used Royce's idealism to give this conviction a philosophical justification. Just like he did with James though, Jones 'Christianized' Royce: Royce's critics complained that his conception of the Absolute was of passive, powerless, passionless Thought, but Jones assumed that the all-encompassing consciousness was the Christian God of love.

The third kindling flame at Harvard was Francis Greenwood Peabody (1847–1936). Peabody was a pioneer of the Social Gospel, a movement that combined the demand for individual transformation with a call to transform society and that would become the dominant expression of Protestantism in America by the end of the first decade of the twentieth century. In 1883 he was the first American theologian to introduce the subject of social reform into the divinity school curriculum, covering issues such as temperance, charity, labour, and prison discipline. He too had an interest in mysticism, believing that the mystic's insight into the divine will was the gift that kept theology fresh. Peabody's ideas and approach would have resonated with Jones' emphasis on action, as demonstrated by his Uncle Eli, for example, and with his interest in mysticism. More generally, the Social Gospel was associated with the belief that it was the responsibility of Christians to establish the Kingdom of God (others believed that Jesus would establish the Kingdom when he returned), a belief that appealed to Jones and that was in line with the liberal strand of Quakerism. Peabody certainly seems to have been popular within some branches of Quakerism: a 1902 Quaker review of his *Jesus Christ and the Social Question* warned that any minister who knowingly neglected it was neglecting his duty. Jones did not study with Peabody, but they became friends, and Jones described him in a letter to Elizabeth as about as near perfect as any man he had ever seen and a remarkable speaker.

To sum up, Peabody, James and Royce gave Jones much food for thought, especially about the implications of consciousness and the subconscious for the human–divine relationship. In the next chapter, we'll look at how Jones interpreted his experience of God in the light of these diverse kindling flames from South China, Haverford and Harvard.

3

The Inner Light: The presence of God

When it came to doing theology, Jones had two very broad guidelines. On the one hand, and in line with other liberal Christians, he was convinced that faith needed to be reformulated in the light of advances in science, philosophy and biblical criticism. On the other, and in line with many Quakers, he was always more concerned with a dynamic Christian life than with abstract speculation. Referring to the fourth-century debates about the nature of Christ, for example, he complained that, 'It is somewhat difficult for a person who has a practical mind and who is eager to see the actual reign of God advanced to have any patience with the Arian battle, which seems to him a futile struggle over dim abstractions.'[1] If we add to this the fact that Jones wrote for a lay audience rather than for academics, we would be right if we suspected that his theology might be a little short on rigour. With this limitation in mind, we'll take a brief look at some of his thoughts about God, Christ, human nature, and the presence of God in humans as the Inner Light.

Jones' view of God was first and foremost that God was characterized by love. This is absolutely central to all of his books. It was in line with his experience from childhood onwards, and it is of course a fundamental theme in the Bible. This God of love, thought Jones, was working to bring about the Kingdom of God on Earth. This was not something that would happen suddenly when Christ returned, as some believed, but was a gradual process, with God drawing people by grace and love. Thus God would work not as a dramatic, outside agency but as a subtle, inner strength. As he put it in *Practical Christianity*, alluding to Elijah's experience in the Old Testament, 'The man who goes to work in the line of his duty finds that the God who did not come in the great forces of nature – wind, earthquake, fire – does come in quieter, and in less striking ways, as the power which makes use of a feeble human instrument.'[2]

This question of whether God works from within or as an outside agency did give Jones something of a theological headache though. Theologians discuss this issue in terms of immanence (God is within) and transcendence (God is outside or above the world). Jones' religious experience fitted with a God who was immanent, and he asserted that the immanence of God is consistent with psychology (because we meet God in the subconscious) and philosophy (because human consciousness is a particular instance of God's consciousness). He was criticized for emphasizing immanence at the expense of transcendence, though, so that everything becomes God – a position known as pantheism. Jones admitted that it was difficult to draw the line between a two-world theory that separated humans and God and an equally dangerous pantheism that named the everything 'God'. But he claimed that in all his books he had been trying to set forth an interpretation of God which brought 'the two worlds' together into a single unity.

Jones also received a lot of criticism for his view of Jesus. Broadly speaking, the problem here is that if humans are related to God through the subconscious, Jesus' traditionally understood role of reconciling humans and God might be redundant. To try to gain some traction on this issue, it is useful to look at two concepts that theologians use when talking about Jesus: the incarnation (referring to the embodiment of God in flesh as a man) and the atonement (the meaning of the death of Jesus). When it comes to the incarnation, Jones is absolutely clear that Jesus was the ultimate revelation of God. Christians have been preoccupied since the fourth century, however, with the question of how Jesus could be both divine and human. Jones identifies the problem as being that almost all theological discussions on the subject start with God and humans as separated. The solution lies in 'modern psychology', he says, which has shown that God is part of human nature. This starting point means that there are no metaphysical difficulties in the way of an actual incarnation of God. It is rather what one would expect. Quite apart from the fact that we might view this claim about what psychology has shown with some scepticism, the obvious question that this creates, and which Jones never really addresses, is whether Jesus is fundamentally (or ontologically, to put it more theologically) any different from the rest of us regarding his divine nature.

When it comes to the atonement, there are a number of explanations of why Jesus died on the cross. Among evangelical Quakers of the time, it was held that we have all sinned so deserve to be punished, but because God is merciful, God visited this deserved punishment on Jesus instead of on us. It is a theory that can be traced back to the ancient Hebrews, when lambs were sacrificed to take away God's wrath. Jones disliked this theory intensely. The purely mechanical view of a transaction that it offers is, he complained, deeply coloured by mythology and by crude ideas of primitive sacrifice. Psychology, he felt, offered a way forward, because it provided a deeper view of human personality and divine personality than was possible when the historic creeds were formulated. It should thus be possible to abandon illustrations drawn from law courts, he said, and come up with conceptions that fit the actual facts of inward, personal experience. Thus, Jones drew on James' discussions of ideals and talked about how Jesus provides us with ideals that are far above those produced by anyone else and that attract us to God.

But if everyone has the same type of relationship with God as Jesus, are the ideals set out by him necessary? Shouldn't we be able to find ideals and God on our own? Jones answers this question using an analogy. Just as someone wanting to know about music would turn to a Mozart or Beethoven rather than to a boy with a harmonica, so the 'supreme education of the soul comes through an intimate acquaintance with Jesus Christ of history'.[3] His explanation admittedly leaves open the possibility of following lesser ideals (cf. learning just a little bit about music), but it is clear that this is very much a second best, and, for all practical purposes, knowledge of Jesus is to be preferred. Unsurprisingly, some evangelical Quakers were unimpressed with Jones' approach, and in *The Trail of Life in the Middle Years*, Jones quotes a letter from one of his 'watchful critics', who informed him in no uncertain terms that, 'Jesus Christ was sent into the world *for no other purpose* but to be offered as a sacrifice for the sins of the whole world by shedding his blood on Calvary.'[4]

Even if we have ideals from Jesus, though, how can we follow them and become better people? Evangelicals, after all, viewed humans as inherently sinful, and most of us know how hard it can be to do what we know we should, even with the best of intentions. Jones' answer again drew on James, and in particular on his chapter on habit in *Principles*. It was a well-known chapter, reputedly preached from a thousand pulpits, and Jones tells of seeing an entire class hushed with solemn awe under its moral power. James writes that habits are formed because of the plasticity of the organic material of which bodies are composed. Thus, in the brain, once a 'nerve-current' has formed a path, the path will follow the law of most of the paths we know and be made stronger with repeated use. James emphasized that this was useful: habits make things easier because each time we do something it requires less effort. (He offered practical suggestions arising from this observation regarding how new habits can be formed; for example, he advised readers never to make an exception until the new habit was securely rooted in their lives.)

Jones discusses this in relation to choosing the good. Drawing an analogy with how writing self-consciously makes the writing lose its grace and flow, he suggests that the aim for individuals is to make the choice of goodness natural rather than strained: 'Happy is the man who not only has won the skill of body by his habitual exercise, but has also by his choices and decision gained a moral dexterity of the soul so that it has become second nature to choose the good!'[5] The deliberate and habitual choice to do good, then, makes a person good. Indeed, we can tell if we have made progress in this field by the ease with which we perform our tasks and duties. It is basically a general statement of the adage that if you want to be a kind person, start by doing kind things. Jones often refers to this transformation in relation to Clement's terminology of the 'harmonized man', namely someone who has brought their soul into parallelism with divine currents, has habitually practised their religious insights, and has finally formed a unified central self, acutely responsive to the Beyond within.

It was thus central to Jones' thought that humans and God are related, and a large part of his legacy is generally taken to be his expression of this belief in terms of the key Quaker concept of the Inward or Inner Light. (Jones favoured the latter terminology, and largely thanks to him it became more prevalent than the former.) In *Social Law in the Spiritual World*, he explains that it was traditionally used by early Quakers in three main ways: to represent (i) a Divine Life resident in the soul; (ii) a source of guidance and illumination; and (iii) a ground of spiritual certitude (i.e., of experience or conviction). The Inner Light is an important concept partly because it is more than just an abstract theological construct. It has implications for behaviour, in that if all people have God within, for example, they should be treated accordingly with love and respect. It also has implications for spiritual practices, in that Bible reading is necessarily approached differently depending on whether one sees the Light as authoritative over the Bible or as an aid to reading it.

Jones' first extended expression of his views on this topic was in the above-mentioned *Social Law in the Spiritual World*, which was written in 1904 (although he had presented his views at various summer schools in the few years previously). The book clearly bears the mark of his studies at Harvard in 1900/01, and he expresses his great debt to Royce and James in the Introduction. However, he also says that the book is deliberately written in a 'popular' rather than a 'scientific' style and will avoid technical terms: in line with this, he justifies his views through broad general references to 'psychology' or 'philosophy' rather than through careful critiques of the thought of these two men.

His main complaint was that the traditional seventeenth-century understanding of the Inner Light was dualistic, having been formulated by the Scottish Quaker theologian Robert Barclay at a time when the dualism of the French philosopher Descartes was prevalent. By this, Jones meant that it had been understood as a supernatural faculty rather than as an inherent part of human nature. Or, as he put it, it had been envisioned as 'foreign' to human nature rather than as something that a 'man has as *man*'. Jones was possibly not representing Barclay fairly here, as a number of scholars have argued that Barclay's views were not quite as dualistic as he and other liberal Quakers of that era made out, but nevertheless a dualistic view was often used as a foil in discussions about the Inner Light. Jones complained that this dualistic view was based on woefully imperfect psychology. Now, he confidently proclaimed, the Inner Light has been shown by psychology and philosophy to be an integral part of human nature.

Inevitably, his radical new formulation initially met with some opposition, with a common objection, especially from evangelical Quakers, being that God did not dwell in souls that were in hell, were unrepentant, or had no faith in Christ. Jones' view gradually gained ground among liberal Quakers, however, and by the 1950s it was predominant.

In the 1920s, Jones' discussions of the relationship between God and humans widened to encompass other religions. He had a memorable meeting with Gandhi in 1926 (the invitation is shown in Figure 3), and wrote to Margaret Jones that the life of the Ashram was very simple and they had talked of Christ and Quakerism as a way of life. A year later, he expressed the hope in *New Studies in Mystical Religion* that one day 'we in the West will learn the secret which India has always possessed – that the soul is the eternally important fact and its testimony the ground of all truth'.[6]

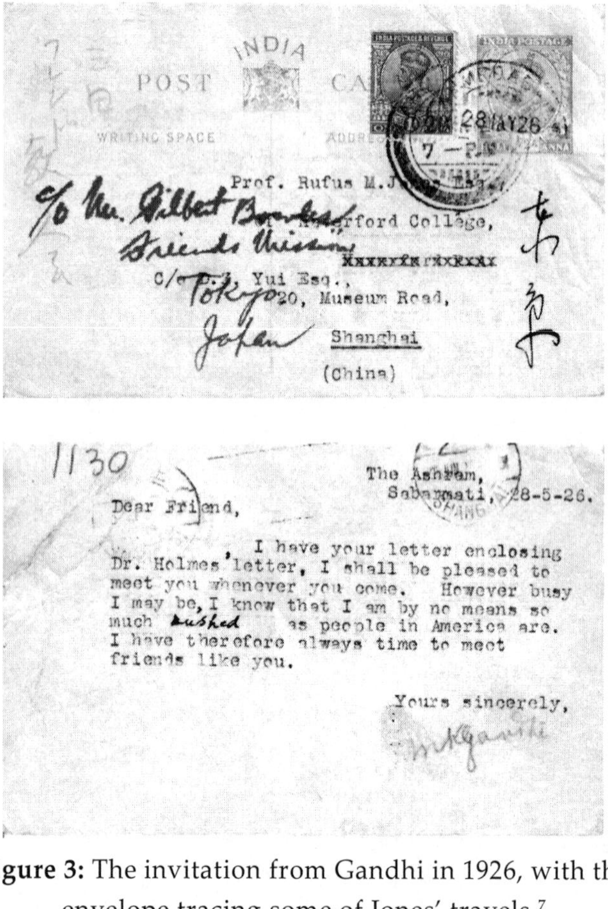

INDIA
POST CARD
WRITING SPACE
ADDRESS

Prof. Rufus M.J
c/o Mr. Gilbert Bowles
rford College,
Friends Mission
C/o Yui Esq.,
Tokyo 20, Museum Road,
Japan Shanghai
(China)

1130

The Ashram,
Sabarmati, 28-5-26.

Dear Friend,

I have your letter enclosing Dr. Holmes' letter, I shall be pleased to meet you whenever you come. However busy I may be, I know that I am by no means so much rushed as people in America are. I have therefore always time to meet friends like you.

Yours sincerely,

MKGandhi

Figure 3: The invitation from Gandhi in 1926, with the envelope tracing some of Jones' travels.[7]

So, are Jones' views convincing? It is an important question, given that they have been so influential. Jones himself seemed absolutely sure that psychology and philosophy supported his views, and he convinced many others. The British Quaker Joan Fry, for example, wrote to Jones shortly after the publication of *Social Law*, enthusing that he had put Quaker views 'quite plainly in the direct line of what one might call philosophical development', and expressing her gratitude that he had shown how 'much that was merely instinctive, is really verified by the slower methods of science'.[8]

We could start by assessing a few of Jones' assumptions and arguments. First of all, we might doubt whether his views offer a good explanation for our human capacity to do both good and evil. If God is good and the basis of human consciousness, for example, we might wonder how people can do things that are decidedly not good. Jones offers practical guidelines for discerning what guidance might be from God and what might not be (as we'll see in Chapter 5), but he doesn't really explain how consciousness and the subconscious can give rise to actions and ideas that are not of God.

We might also conclude that Jones' evidence for the existence of a universal relationship between humans and God is a bit thin. He says that psychology supports his formulation of the Inner Light, but there were plenty of psychologists who did not believe that humans met God in the subconscious, and indeed many were atheists. Furthermore, he draws on Royce and James without really addressing how their views of God differed from his. In *The Trail of Life in the Middle Years*, he insists that he did not adopt Royce's system of thought as his own, and in *Pathways to the Reality of God*, he clarifies that 'I am not here endorsing James' well-known conception of God which I do not share, I am only borrowing some of his luminous phrases to help supply vivid imagery for making God as Spirit *real* to our minds'.[9] But he does not provide any details in either case. Given that both men were such a big influence on him, and that the views of many Quakers today have more in common with James' 'more' than with Jones' view of God, this is a shame. Neither does he address how the views of James and Royce differed from each other. These differences ran deep though. Following Royce's Gifford lectures, for example, James wrote a critique that Royce responded to in a 23-page letter, and when James was preparing his own Gifford lectures, he wrote to Royce that he was doing so in the exclusive hope of overthrowing Royce's idealism and ruining his peace! In part, as we saw above, this lack of rigour was deliberate, because *Social Law* was written for the 'wayfaring man' who wanted to understand the latest insights but couldn't because the existing books were too technical. It does, however, mean that Jones' ideas about the Inner Light do not have strong foundations.

In addition to looking at these problems with Jones' arguments, it is also useful to look at the criticisms that have been made of his ideas over the years, by both scholars and Quakers. First of all, he is often criticized for having too optimistic a view of human nature. In the first years of the twentieth century, his views were not unusual. They were in line with the wider Christian liberal optimism of the time, and they were also in line with the positive view of human nature that was inherent to a greater or lesser extent in Quakerism because of its emphasis on the Inner Light. Jones said that he was inspired by the view of his Haverford teacher Pliny Chase, for example, who taught that each individual was given new glory and a noble dignity because the nucleus of their life was in touch with Eternal Reality. In later years, the two world wars gave many pause for thought, and Jones was no exception. No doubt referring to his meeting with the Gestapo (see Chapter 1), he wrote that, 'We have seen in new and awful light in our times how low in the scale man can sink ... I personally saw and dealt with the most debased men in the list. Christ saw a similar depravity in man [but] He kept His hope and His faith that God and man belonged together, as branches belong to a vine.'[10] What is interesting about this comment is that it suggests that Jones' optimism about human nature was based not on his view of humans *per se*, but on his opinion of the relationship between humans and God.

A related accusation (and it often is an accusation, in the sense that it is seen as going against traditional Christian beliefs) is that Jones was a humanist, and that, because of his influence, today's Quakerism is humanistic. There are no doubt several reasons for this criticism, but perhaps one is that, as we have seen above, Jones recognized that a lot of effort was involved in becoming a good person: like excellence in any field, he said, it costs labour and toil and is the fruit of concentration and persistent effort. Jones himself, though, consistently asserted that he was opposed to humanism because it reduced humans to natural beings, and he claimed that it was impossible for someone to lift themselves by their own belt into a life of consummate truth and beauty. Although our efforts are good and our moral enthusiasms noble, there is a cosmic free grace working for us, he insisted, and our best line of action is to align ourselves with it.

A further criticism that is often raised is that he sees the possibility of direct personal experience of God as based on the nature and psychology of humans, whereas, traditionally, Quakers saw it as based on the supernatural activity of God. Jones did, however, lose some of his enthusiasm for psychology in later years. He recognized that Freud and Jung had shown that the subconscious contained hissing serpents as well as glorious birds of paradise, as he put it, and in 1921 he wrote a rare academic article titled 'Psychology and the spiritual life' in *Journal of Religion* critiquing the way psychology had developed. Essentially, he was something of a fair-weather friend to psychology: he drew on it in very general terms when it fitted his experience of a sense of God's presence, but he ignored it or criticized it when it did not! Furthermore, from what we have seen of Jones' motivation, it seems that he wasn't trying to replace God's supernatural activity with a psychological understanding of humans. Rather, he was seeking to show that God's activity within was explicable through psychology, which in turn would make faith credible for those who might be doubting. If we keep his aim in mind, then this criticism seems particularly ironic.

From these brief comments, what is probably clear is that Jones needs to be interpreted and criticized with some caution. We need to take into account the fact that he wrote informally, keep in mind what he was trying to do, and assess his work as a whole, because, for example, he sometimes stresses the need to put effort into becoming good in one place, and the role of God's help in this venture somewhere else.

As a final comment, it is worth pointing out that the fact that there are holes in Jones' arguments does not necessarily mean that he was on completely the wrong track – just that he needed to do a bit more work and/or wait for further progress in our knowledge of consciousness. I suspect that if he were alive today, he would have been fascinated and inspired by the ideas of Iain McGilchrist, who, like Jones, thinks very highly of James. McGilchrist is widely recognized as a polymath, with particular expertise in psychiatry, neuroimaging and philosophy, and a particular interest in how the right and left hemispheres of our brain attend to the world in different ways. Broadly speaking, the left hemisphere enables us to break things down into their constituent parts and manipulate them, whereas the right hemisphere enables us to see the bigger picture and to appreciate art, beauty, and spirituality. Problems occur, he explains in *The Master and his Emissary* (2009), when the way the left hemisphere perceives reality becomes dominant, as it is in the West, because we lose much that is of value. Jones, who valued both science and poetry, and both logic and intuition, would have recognized McGilchrist's assessment of today's situation, I am sure. Perhaps of more fundamental significance, though, is that Jones felt that consciousness could never be explained by science – it is elementary and unanalyzable and its origins are a mystery. He surmised that one day it would be discovered that 'what we have been calling "physical" or "material" or "molecular" is vastly more interpenetrated by "spirit" than we have usually supposed'.[11] McGilchrist discusses consciousness in his 1500-page epic *The Matter with Things* (2021), where he argues at length that although consciousness and matter interact, consciousness is more fundamental, with some form of consciousness being present in all matter. One consequence of matter being imbued with a sort of consciousness or 'spirit' is that it affects how we view the role and function of the brain. Jones, for his part, felt that consciousness was mediated, rather than produced, by the brain. And along similar lines, McGilchrist argues that the brain acts as a kind of filter, 'sculpting' consciousness by saying 'no' to some things and allowing others to stand forward into being. Perhaps Jones would have built on these ideas to argue that 'sin' or 'evil' occur when we say 'no' to the consciousness that is the Christian God of love. Perhaps he would have understood experiences of God as occurring when the filter on consciousness acts as it should and lets God through. This approach would certainly resonate with his comments about the need to align oneself with divine currents.

Leaving speculation aside and returning to the early twentieth century, though, Jones' views gained ground, in spite of their flaws. This was perhaps partly because he expressed the idea that God is part of human nature in terms of mysticism. It was a topic that was of huge interest at the time, as we will see in the next chapter.

4

Mysticism: Practising the presence

The word *mystica* came into Christianity through the fifth-century Syrian monk known as Pseudo-Dionysius the Areopagite. It derives from the Greek term *mu*, which has connotations of secrecy (as in the phrase 'keeping mum'). For Pseudo-Dionysius, mystical theology involved secrecy of mind, or a state of consciousness beyond knowing that experienced God as 'a ray of the Divine Dark'. His writings surfaced in the sixth century, were translated into Latin by John Scotus Erigena in the ninth, and proved to be enormously influential within the Western monastic tradition from the twelfth century onwards. The anonymous author of the fourteenth-century classic *The Cloud of Unknowing*, for example, gives the following advice to his 'friend in God': 'Reconcile yourself to wait in this darkness as long as is necessary, but still go on longing after him whom you love. For if you are to feel him or to see him in this life, it must always be in this cloud, in this darkness.'[1] Thus 'mystical theology' came to refer to a way of life involving prayer, contemplation, and self-denial. The word 'mysticism' did not come into use until the mid-eighteenth century, when it was associated with unregulated spiritual impulses and fanaticism and carried connotations of misplaced sexuality.

In spite of the fact that the Church did not always embrace mysticism, concerned that unmediated, imageless communion with God might make it redundant or lead people astray, in the early twentieth century mysticism captured the public imagination to the extent that a writer in the *Church Quarterly Review* in 1906 declared that the United States was a country in which mysticism and a craving for spiritual experiences had 'run mad'. So what happened to make mysticism respectable?

The process started in 1856 with Vaughan's *Hours*, which had so captivated the young Jones, as we saw in Chapter 2. In the following decades, the Transcendentalists (the movement associated with Emerson) played a vital role and loosened mysticism's ties with Christianity. William James also gave the mystic cause a significant boost in *Varieties*, conferring scientific credibility on religious experience and, in line with the Transcendentalists, claiming that religious feelings are almost always the same for Stoic, Christian, and Buddhist saints. Furthermore, religious liberals recognized that mysticism offered a refuge from an increasingly scientific and materialistic worldview, and, finally, simple curiosity about other religions seems to have played a role, as sacred writings were beginning to be translated into English.

Jones' conviction after reading Emerson at college that his early religious experiences were mystical, coupled with his psychological and philosophical explorations of the inherent relationship between humans and God, inevitably meant that he would be an enthusiastic participant in the conversation about mysticism. To take just a few examples of his books, in *Studies in Mystical Religion* (1909) he focuses on the mystics that he believed were the forerunners of Quakerism: there are chapters on Plato, Plotinus, the Church Fathers, St Francis, and the Anabaptists, among others. (His view that Quakerism arose out of continental mysticism has, however, since been discredited.) In *New Studies in Mystical Religion* (1927), he discusses mysticism as it relates to the abnormal, asceticism, and religious education. And in *The Luminous Trail* (1947), written when in his eighties, he describes an eclectic selection of saints, whether canonized or not, whom he deemed to have been 'open-windowed' to God. Thus, while there are stalwarts such as Paul, John, and Francis of Assisi, the final chapter considers his son Lowell. Jones was of the opinion that 'his life was so full of promise, the attitude of direction was so marked, that I am convinced he belongs in my list here'.[2]

Jones also counted the most prominent scholars of mysticism as good friends. Chief among these were Evelyn Underhill, a respected Anglo-Catholic retreat leader and author of the classic *Mysticism* (1911), and William Ralph Inge (1860–1954), often referred to as Dean Inge because of his position from 1911 to 1934 as Dean of St Paul's Cathedral.

Jones and Underhill disagreed at times. Jones seemed frustrated by Underhill's failure to grasp Quaker spirituality, complaining in a letter to his friend Violet Holdsworth that 'she is quite unable to appreciate or even to understand the full meaning of Quaker worship without sacraments',[3] but he nonetheless described her as a 'great soul'. They also differed about the value of unusual phenomena such as St Francis' stigmata (the phenomenon of experiencing bleeding palms, reflecting what happened to Jesus as he was crucified). In a later edition of *Mysticism*, Underhill takes issue with Jones' assertion that stigmata were the marks of emotional and physical abnormality. She counters that a flame of living love that for one dazzling instant welded body and soul together was hardly a point of weakness in a saint. The letter from Underhill in Figure 4 acknowledges that the two of them did see the saints from different angles, and expresses relief that Jones was not displeased by anything she said about his book *New Studies*.

Inge and his wife enjoyed a visit to the Joneses at Haverford in the early 1920s, during which Jones and Inge gave lectures at the Bellevue-Stratford hotel in Philadelphia. Rufus Jones folklore holds that Jones, sensitive to the habits of his English guest, secretly cleaned the shoes that Inge left outside his door every night, accepting without comment the tip Inge asked him to give to the boy who cleaned them so well, but Jones denied it. He did, however, reveal that they wandered around the maze of corridors in the Bellevue for some time searching for their hats and coats before Inge (who was known for his dry sense of humour) smiled and suggested, 'Don't you think we had better get a non-mystical person to guide us?'[5]

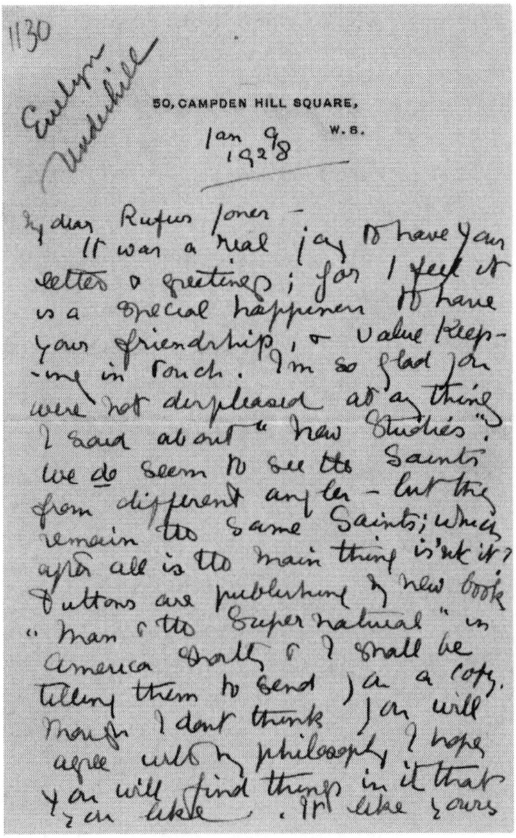

1130

Evelyn Underhill

50, CAMPDEN HILL SQUARE, W.8.

Jan 9 1928

My dear Rufus Jones –
It was a real joy to have your letter & greetings; for I feel it is a special happiness to have your friendship, & value keeping in touch. I'm so glad you were not displeased at anything I said about "New Studies". We do seem to see the Saints from different angles – but they remain the same Saints; which after all is the main thing isn't it? Duttons are publishing my new book "Man & the Supernatural" in America shortly & I shall be telling them to send you a copy. Though I don't think you will agree with my philosophy, I hope you will find things in it that you like. It's like yours

Figure 4: Extract of a letter to Jones from Evelyn Underhill, 9 January 1928, referring to their different views of the saints.[4]

For all this interest, mysticism remained a notoriously woolly term, and Jones once commented that at the end of any lecture on the subject someone would be sure to rise and ask, 'Will the speaker kindly tell us in two or three plain words what mysticism really is?'[6] He complained that the word was often used to connote spurious knowledge, occult lore, or abnormal phenomena, such that it stood for claptrap and mental rubbish.

For Jones, though, mysticism was fundamentally an experience of God. As he put it in *Social Law*, a mystic is someone who '*feels* his relationship to the Infinite'.[7] More specifically, this mystical experience is one of personal relationship with a God who is 'a warm and intimate Person whose reality makes our hearts tingle, and who sends us forth with thrill and enthusiasm for high adventure and infinite hazard'.[8] Related to this, a mystical religion is a religion that puts the emphasis on immediate awareness of a relationship with God.

But is everyone able to experience this sense of divine presence? Jones seemed to struggle at times over the answer to this. The fact that the 'shekinah of the soul', as he put it, is in the subconscious suggests that experience of God should be universal, and in most of his writings Jones insists that fellowship with God is as normal a trait of human life as breathing. The prominent Quaker William Littleboy, however, took Jones gently to task in a letter in 1912, pointing out that many devout and sincere Quakers did not possess this spiritual consciousness. Perhaps in response to this, Jones acknowledges in *Spiritual Reformers*, published two years later in 1914, that the ability to have a mystical experience was dependent on the psychic structure of the inner self.

Part of the problem here seems to be in agreeing on what is meant by spiritual consciousness and on what experiences qualify as 'mystical'. Littleboy may have felt that he lacked an awareness of God's presence, but he certainly found a sense of peace in his faith. In his eloquent 1916 pamphlet 'The Appeal of Quakerism to the Non-Mystic', he assured his readers that if they followed Jesus and tried to love others with the generosity and forgiveness of God then they too would experience a calm certitude: 'Your whole life will be illuminated, and though no ecstasy be yours, you shall have the peace that comes of the assurance that God is yours and you are His.'[9] The question, then, is whether Jones would have classified Littleboy's sense of peace as mystical. The answer, I think, is 'yes'. If we trawl through Jones' writings we can find descriptions of various types of religious experience, and in fact they map quite well onto the six types identified more formally by Caroline Davis in her book *The Evidential Force of Religious Experience*.[10] Davis only classifies one of these types of experience as 'mystical', but Jones would put them all under the mystical umbrella. We'll look at them below.

(1) *Interpretive experience*: This as an experience that is viewed as religious not because of any unusual features of the experience itself but because it is interpreted within a religious framework, such as taking an event to be the answer to prayer. For Jones, all life is potentially an interpretive religious experience, because God is intrinsically bound up with the world. The life of a mystic, he says, 'is always like the palimpsest which bears in underlying writing a sacred text ... The slenderest human task becomes glorious because God is in it.'[11] In other words, there is no line between the secular and the sacred, so all experiences can be interpreted as religious.

(2) *Quasi-sensory experience*: This is a religious experience in which the main element is a physical sensation or one that involves a 'quasi-sensory' event, such as a vision, dream, or voice. Jones was generally distrustful of experiences of this type. Although he appreciated that many curious phenomena could be explained by the operations of the subconscious, he said he trusted them only so far as they could be tested and verified. In fact, he made a point of resolutely ignoring an audition he experienced on one occasion. Describing how he was making final preparations a few days before an important address about which he was nervous, he recounts that, 'As I took the manuscript from the drawer of my desk, I distinctly heard a voice say to me, "But thou wilt never give it!" I was so startled by the voice that I dropped the paper and looked around to see if anyone could have spoken, and

I even went into the hall, wondering whether the voice was from the outside or from within.'[12] During the night before the scheduled address, Jones and his hosts came down with severe food poisoning. Jones was hospitalized, but, against all the odds, was allowed out of bed an hour before the talk was due to start, and somehow managed to address an audience of nearly a thousand. As he reflected on the voice at a later date, he wrote that instead of depressing him and inclining him to surrender to the inevitable, it made him even more determined to fulfil his obligation. He concluded that the audition was due not to a divine initiation but to a subconscious morbid impulse of a tired man.

(3) *Revelatory experience*: This is an experience that includes a sudden conviction, inspiration or enlightenment. Jones embraced these types of experience, and in fact viewed them as a natural phenomenon akin to the way any 'genius' experiences a moment of intuition (think of the spiritual authority he gave to poets, for example). In the highest creative moments of a genius, he says, there are 'uprushes from below, invasions from regions beyond the ordinary self'.[13]

(4) *Regenerative experience*: This is a frequent type of religious experience among ordinary people, through which they experience new hope, strength, comfort and peace. These experiences can be mild daily occurrences or extraordinary one-off events. In line with this, Jones wrote that the great mystics may gain vision and strength to transform society, and that ordinary people can experience peace in everyday life. Jones himself had a profound, if not dramatic, experience of regeneration after being knocked down by a car. (He broke three ribs and his leg and tore ligaments, but continued to teach his students in his study, lying flat on his back on a hospital bed with his leg in a cast.) He recounts that after his long convalescence he realized that physical healing had been accompanied by spiritual restoration: 'Spiritual energies of a more or less permanent

order flowed in and operated, as though God at my fountains far off had been raining.'[14]

(5) *Numinous experience*: Initially defined by the German scholar Rudolf Otto, a numinous experience involves a sense of awe and 'otherness' but also a fascination and attraction to the divine, or numen. Jones' personal experience that comes closest to belonging in this category is the one, mentioned in Chapter 1, that occurred during a walk at Dieulefit in the Alps. 'Suddenly I felt the walls between the visible and the invisible grow thin and the Eternal seemed to break through into the world where I was,' he wrote. 'I went down on my knees there in the woods with that same feeling of awe which compelled men in earlier times to take off their shoes from their feet.' Significantly, the experience was not an end in itself, however, but was accompanied by a conviction about the future course of his life. He went on to say that, 'A sense of mission broke in on me and I felt that I was being called to a well-defined task of life to which I then and there dedicated myself.'[15]

(6) *Mystical experience*: These experiences include an apprehension of ultimate reality, a sense of freedom from the limitations of time, space and individual ego, or a sense of 'oneness' and bliss or serenity. Jones had an experience that fits some elements of this description, a deeply personal one that occurred while he was at sea on his way to England, not knowing that Lowell was dying back home in America. 'I suddenly felt myself surrounded by an enfolding Presence and held as though by invisible Arms,' he wrote. Again, though, the importance of this experience was not the feeling itself but the strength it imparted, as he went on to affirm that, 'My entire being was fortified and I was inwardly prepared to meet the message of sorrow which was awaiting me next day at the dock.'[16]

Mysticism for Jones clearly covers a wide range of religious experiences. As a summary of his position, which covers both his beliefs and his personal experience, we could do worse than refer to his testimony in *The Trail of Life in the Middle Years*:

> God is more truly like our spirits than like anything else in the universe, not remote, or absentee, close as breathing, the normal environment of the soul, and therefore a real Presence to be found and known and loved, as the swimmer finds the ocean. And this attitude of faith may rise, as it does with me in my best and sanest moments, to a joyous consciousness of acquaintance, fellowship and love. Sometimes it is a flash of sudden insight, sometimes it is a quiet assurance, sometimes it is an unspeakable joy in living, sometimes it is a dim awareness of a resource to live by and to draw upon for action.[17]

From the above quotation and Jones' descriptions of his own religious experiences above, one point that stands out is his conviction that mystical experiences provide strength, guidance and insight, and therefore should lead to action. They should also lead to transformation. Individuals are transformed through their closeness to God: the highest traits of character we know in God are love, gentleness, tenderness and self-giving grace, he says, and the meeting of the soul with God will bring forth such fruits in the life of a person. In tandem with this, society is transformed because both the great mystics and ordinary people find that visions of service open before them.

It is this emphasis on action and service that prompted Jones to identify two types of mystics. A negation mystic is, according to Jones, someone whose goal is to become absorbed in God. This type of mystic holds that God cannot be found in objects, or events in history, or states of consciousness, because these are all finite. They thus aim to transcend the finite, even their own 'self'. It is a type of mysticism that harks back to Pseudo-Dionysius, and as an example Jones cites the thirteenth-century

German mystic Meister Eckhart, whose goal was to experience states of consciousness that approached a blank.

Jones has two objections to this type of mysticism. The first is Eckhart's mistaken belief that whatever comes from beyond consciousness must necessarily come from God. Interestingly, as we saw in the previous chapter, this accusation could actually be made in relation to Jones' own theory of how God and humans are related through consciousness. The second is that it encourages individuals to live for a rare moment of ecstasy and to sacrifice the chance of winning spiritual victory for the hope of receiving an ineffable illumination that would quench all further search or desire. In other words, Jones seems to view negation mysticism as selfish and self-indulgent because its goal is an overwhelming personal experience rather than the provision of strength to overcome sin or a vision to serve others.

Affirmation mystics also seek an immediate, first-hand sense of God, but, in contrast to negation mystics, as a prelude to action and not as an end in itself. It is a mysticism of everyday life in the sense that God is found not by negating the finite but *in* the finite. As we've seen, all human tasks can become 'glorious' because God is in them. Affirmation mysticism involves transformation of will and character, Jones explains, such that 'instead of losing our will we approach that true freedom where we *will* to do His will'.[18]

So, in line with Jones' ideas about the universality of mystical experience, both negation and affirmation mysticism involve an experience of God. His distinction between them rests on how and where the mystic thinks God can be encountered and on what the mystic does based on that experience. Rather confusingly, however, Jones thinks that *in practice* the boundaries between negation mysticism and affirmation mysticism are often blurred, because negation mystics, in spite of their insistence that God cannot be found in anything created, still perform good deeds: 'The great mystics have always saved themselves by neglecting to be consistent with this rigorous negation and abstraction. In their practice they have cut through their theory and gone on living the rich concrete life.'[19] This blurring of boundaries might be why his terminology has not been taken up by scholars more generally. One possible resolution to this paradox, which Jones himself does not consider, may lie in the fact that spiritual practices that go beyond words or knowledge (for example, some forms of meditation), and that are therefore associated with negation mysticism, could in and of themselves make the practitioner more compassionate (see Chapter 5) such that they live the 'rich concrete life' that Jones associated with affirmation mysticism.

In summary, if we take a step back from the broad and occasionally troublesome label of mysticism, we can say that Jones felt that the presence of God should be manifested in everyday life. One way to move away from 'mystical' terminology is to look instead at how we might describe his faith, and a starting point might be to characterize it as experiential, credible, expectant and holistic. It was *experiential* in that it was rooted in his childhood experiences of family worship that enabled God to become a palpable presence. And he was surely speaking from first-hand experience when he proclaimed that, 'A man can face anything when he knows absolutely that at bottom the universe is not force nor mechanism but intelligent and loving purpose, and that through the seeming confusion and welter there is a loving, throbbing, personal Heart answering back to us.'[20]

Although this experience was primary, and at time made proofs of God's existence redundant because God is known at an experiential, deep level to exist, Jones felt that it was also important that faith was *credible*. We have seen how he set about trying to achieve this through engaging with psychology and philosophy, and even if we might harbour some doubts about how well he succeeded, perhaps what is important is that he addressed the issues of the day in enough detail to satisfy his own mind and to be helpful to many others.

His faith was *expectant* in that he felt it was imperative to have high expectations of God. He wrote that, 'Expectation, which is another name for faith, is essential for any high achievement, and of course is peculiarly important in this supreme adventure of the soul.'[21] In order to experience this expectation, it is essential to have right ideas about God. One can hardly expect to get great flushes of love and power, he points out, from believing ever so valiantly in some dim and cloudy Great Mystery, wholly out of the sphere and range of human experience.

Jones' faith could also be described as *holistic*, in the sense that he refused to see it as separate from everyday life and intellectual beliefs. There should be no reason to choose between 'the Church' and 'the world', between 'faith' and 'reason', or between 'the sacred' and 'the secular', he said, and indeed the tendency to assume that we are shut up in an either-or selection keeps us from winning the full richness of the life that is possible for us. In *Spiritual Energies in Daily Life*, Jones illustrates how this attitude might play out in practice with reference to Jesus' parable of the wedding feast.[22] A man sends out wedding invitations, but the prospective guests offer excuses for various reasons: one has just got married, and another has business matters he must attend to, for example. Jones explains that the feast represents the 'true good' and the 'highest blessedness of life'. The mistake lies in treating the wedding feast and obligations of life as rivals. The recently married man would ultimately have been happier if he had responded, 'I have just married a wife and therefore I am peculiarly glad to come to thy feast, since fellowship with thee will make my love more real.' Likewise, the business man would ultimately have benefitted if he had responded, 'I have bought five yoke of oxen, and therefore I want to come to thy divine feast so that I may learn how to turn all I possess into the channels of real service and to make these things which thou hast given me help me find the way to the highest joy and blessedness of life.'

In line with this holistic approach, Jones frequently stressed that social action and spiritual practices belonged together insofar as social action needed to have a tangible divine 'feel' to it. Religious activity that lacked divine inspiration was busy and nervous, or thin and weak, he felt, and lacked the depth and serenity that come from the penetrating, co-operating presence of God. But how exactly do we create the conditions for this to happen? In the final chapter, we'll look at some of the practices that Jones felt were important for cultivating the presence of God.

5

A way of surprise and wonder: Cultivating the presence

Jones' biographer Elizabeth Vining described him as the embodiment of optimism, radiant serenity and unbounded energy, and Jones saw these qualities as a natural outcome of a religion of life. Living becomes buoyant and joyous, he says, and there comes to the soul a calm and serenity that is unusual in restless beings like ourselves. Not only that, but mysticism should make us '100 horsepower' people. It sounds an appealing way to live. Can we learn anything from Jones about how to attain this life of serene vitality?

There are a number of reasons why we might be hesitant. Not many of us, for example, spent our formative years in an immersive yet unoppressive religious atmosphere like that experienced by Jones. Furthermore, Jones was visionary, determined, curious, an extrovert, and a natural leader, which likely affected the way his spiritual life developed. Not all of us can lay claim to these character traits, and nor should we aspire to – each of us is unique and has our own gifts and path to follow. Quakerism too, especially in Britain, is very different from in Jones' time, in that many Quakers do not share Jones' Christian beliefs, so are unlikely to be inspired by his faith.

A further issue is that Jones, in spite of writing numerous books on mysticism, provides very little in the way of specific instruction that might be useful for the aspiring mystic. This is partly because, in contrast to his contemporary Evelyn Underhill, who mapped out a spiritual pathway involving specific stages and practices, Jones happily concluded that the practices of the likes of St John of the Cross were too dry and removed from everyday life to be satisfactory ways to the heart of divine reality. The mystical way, he says, will always remain a way of 'surprise and wonder rather than a beaten and regimented road of travel with a Baedeker guide-book'.[1]

Practical Christianity, for example, is a book consisting of a selection of his editorials that was first published in 1899 and in an expanded edition in 1905. In the Introduction, Jones says that its aim was to emphasize the importance of 'practising the presence of God'. He returns again and again to a handful of themes: Christianity must be applied to life because active service strengthens faith; every Christian needs an awareness of God's presence; the formulation of Christianity has to change according to current thought; and the essence of the Gospel is the parable of the prodigal son because God draws us to Himself. It is not, however, a handbook of techniques.

He also makes a few general comments in *The Luminous Trail*, a book that he says is about persons whose lives have revealed their experience of the presence of the living God. Here he identifies four 'highroads of the soul' that are apparent in the Bible. The first is the Road to Damascus, on which we experience a spiritual awakening (Saul of Tarsus famously encountered the risen Christ on the way to Damascus, a watershed experience that saw him go from persecuting to leading Christians). The second is the spirit of the Jerusalem Road of complete commitment, as when Jesus was determined to go to Jerusalem even though he knew that crucifixion awaited him. The third is the Jericho Road of service, as in the parable in which a Samaritan helped a wounded traveller on the way to Jericho. The fourth is the Emmaus Road of fellowship with Christ, from the biblical story of when two of the disciples travelling to Emmaus talked with the risen Christ without recognizing him. But again, he does not translate these 'highroads' into specific advice.

Jones did, however, have a wide range of what we might classify as spiritual practices (think of his childhood times of family silence, for example). The difficulty is that most can be identified only through tantalizing glimpses into his life revealed in his autobiographies. At least seven are apparent though, and so in this final chapter we'll look at what Jones said about them and at how they were expressed in his own life. I've also included a few suggestions for how we might incorporate these practices in our own lives – mainly as references to books and, in the tradition of the Quaker *Advices and Queries*, in the form of questions to ponder.

For some, I've also included a pointer to recent scientific research that suggests how that particular practice might be beneficial for our well-being. I do this with some hesitation, because I think Jones would have objected to reducing spirituality to well-being in the same way as he objected to reducing religion to good works – both well-being and religious activity for him needed to be shot through with the Divine. That said, I think he would have appreciated seeing a scientific basis for the benefits of religious practices. He did, after all, see the world as fundamentally spiritual, which suggests that we should *expect* science to endorse life-giving religious practices. Indeed, science was beginning to investigate such practices in his own time, and rather than finding it threatening (for example, because it might somehow disprove the existence of God), he was thankful for it. Recognizing that prayer had a psychologically explainable subjective aspect, for instance, he wrote that, 'We may well be grateful for all those features of life that can be brought under well-known laws and can be explained by principles with which we have grown familiar.' He continued, however, that 'there is much more involved in the experience and power of prayer than can be attributed to its subjective effects'.[2]

Taken together, the practices below touch on many aspects of human nature – they encompass not only what we might characterize as our spiritual side, but also our intellect, our relationships with nature and with other people, our talents, and our approach to suffering.

5.1 Quaker meeting for worship

There is some subtle telepathy that comes into play in the living silence of a congregation which makes every earnest seeker more quick to feel the presence of God, more acute of inner ear, more tender of heart to feel the bubbling of the springs of life than any one of them would be in isolation ... If this is so, if each assists all and all in turn assist each, our responsibilities in meetings for worship are very real and very great and we must try to realize that there is a form of ministry which is dynamic even when the lips are sealed.[3]

Quaker practice has always revolved around times of silence, in which the communal aspect is paramount. To view meetings as a time for individual meditation would be to miss the point. Jones seemed to see meetings as embodying group affirmation mysticism, in that they involved both a felt experience of God and an opportunity for discerning God's guidance for action in the world.

Regarding the experience of God, he wrote that, 'In our best moments of hush and quiet, especially in those high-tide occasions when many hearts together are fused in silent communion, there often is a palpitating sense of divine presence, an overbrimming consciousness of healing, vivifying currents of life circulating underneath our little lives, and we are thereupon filled with joy and wonder.'[4] Furthermore, the atmosphere created by the group can help each individual to feel the presence of God, presumably in the same way that it did when he was a child, in the moments when he was swept up in the experience of his elders.

Regarding guidance, Jones believed that the group had an essential role in bringing clarity. Just as an 'ordinary painter' needs to exhibit their work so that others can discern whether or not it is great, he explains, so ordinary people must test their leadings by the spiritual life of others. But just how does the group go about testing a leading? Jones mentions a number of criteria. There should be *consistency with orthodox doctrine*, for example. While individuals test their ideas by the revelation of the group, the group, in turn, should test its faith and spirit by the wider revelation that has come through prophets and apostles and saints and martyrs. It is also important to *assess the spiritual health of the group*, because 'If the meeting is rent by faction or is disturbed by stubborn and self-guided members the spiritual method fails to work perfectly'.[5] Ultimately, however, guidance is to be judged by the so-called *fruits criterion*, in that we need to ask whether obedience to this prompting will 'construct not only a better person, but a better social group, a truer and a diviner fellowship'.[6]

Meetings that might be described as 'mystical', in the sense that the group as a whole is particularly aware of God's presence and God seems to be speaking clearly, are often described within the Quaker community as 'gathered'. The exposition *par excellence* of this phenomenon, and one which brings the mystical dimension to the fore, is that given by Thomas Kelly, a friend and colleague of Jones at Haverford. In a short essay titled 'The Gathered Meeting', he writes that, 'In the practice of group worship on the basis of silence come special times when the electric hush and solemnity and depth of power steals over the worshipers ... The burning bush has been kindled in our midst, and we stand together on holy ground.'[7] The meeting may be silent, or may be characterized by several individuals speaking, drawing out a theme, but in such a way that vocal contributions enhance the spiritual atmosphere rather than merely breaking the silence: the silence and words are of 'one texture, one piece'.[8] William James, who as we have seen studied mysticism and religious experience extensively, described a mystic state of an individual as exhibiting four characteristics, and Kelly claims that these characteristics apply to a gathered meeting too: such experiences are ineffable (they need to be experienced and cannot be described), noetic (they appear to give insights beyond the intellect), transient (they rarely last longer than half an hour), and passive (although a mystical experience may be facilitated by focusing the attention, for example, once in the mystic state, an individual will feel as if their own will is temporarily suspended).[9]

Given that everyone in a Quaker meeting can contribute to an atmosphere that creates the conditions for it to be 'gathered', Jones emphasized that we have a great responsibility for worship. It is a responsibility that can perhaps be met partly by following some of the practices outlined below.

Suggestions

Quaker readers will be familiar with meetings for worship, although the fact that many Quakers today are not Christians inevitably changes the interpretation of what is happening, if not the experience itself. Beliefs notwithstanding, it might be useful to ask what helps you prepare to be receptive to whatever may emerge in a meeting, and what makes it difficult to centre down and be still. What difference do practical considerations make (mode of transport, what you do beforehand, how early you arrive)? What helps you to prepare spiritually throughout the week? Non-Quaker readers who would like to try out this form of communal silence, incidentally, can be assured of a warm welcome and should be able to find a local meeting online.

The book by Thomas Kelly is *The Eternal Promise* (Friends United Press, 2006).

5.2 Prayer, silence and reflection

Persons who pray in living faith, in some way unlock reservoirs of energy and release great sources of power within their interior depths.[10]

Times of hush and meditation, 'recollection' and integration, bring resources to live by as well as health and restoration. Serenity comes not alone by removing the outward causes and occasions of fear, but by the discovery of inward reservoirs of strength to draw upon.[11]

Prayer, said Jones, is the highest activity of the soul, providing a deep constructive energy of life that is essential to spiritual health and growth. It is a personal meeting of the soul with God, bringing the joy of communion. It is also a mystery, as difficult to explain as our joy over love and beauty. Fortunately, he says, we do not need to understand vital processes before we utilize them and start living by them.

Jones identifies various types of prayer. One type involves union or communion with God in silence, and he sometimes refers to this rather loosely as meditation. Terminology aside, he says that, 'When we learn how to center down into the stillness and quiet, to listen with our souls for the whisperings of Life and Truth, to bring all our inner powers into parallelism with the set of divine currents, we shall hear tidings from the inner world at the heart and center of which is God.'[12] In line with this, he talks about a flash of insight that would often come for a sermon during a period of silence. And he describes how he would sometimes finish a period of meditation knowing what course of action to take: 'I have many times risen from a period of intense meditation with a difficult decision suddenly made, and at such times I have had no knowledge of the arguments or the steps that led me to the decision. It seemed to roll out ready made, or to be handed to me "from deeper in".'[13]

He also talks about intercessory prayer, or asking God to do things. Here there are a few caveats. For one thing, there are many things that should not be prayed for – prayer should certainly not be used for selfish gratification, for example. Nor should it be used as an excuse not to act – we shouldn't pray for our country on election day and then go off fishing without casting a vote. We should not pray for things that dishonour God either – the common practice of asking God to be loving or present, for example, dishonours God because it is asking God to be true to God's nature. It is like asking lead to be heavy. Jones also expresses some doubt about the efficacy of asking God to act on inanimate things, or in areas where cause follows effect. He is confident, however, that in the realm of personal relationships we can throw ourselves unperplexed on God, believing that what we pray for affects the heart of God and influences the course and current of the Deeper Life that makes the world. Furthermore, requests to God should originate in a transformative relationship with God, because it is only as a person enters more deeply into the life of the Spirit that they see the true things to ask for, so that an increase in the power of prayer is a good barometer of spiritual growth.

Regarding praying in public, Jones was wary of prayers that were written more for an audience than for God. But he said he found short prayers useful, especially those that asked for more light, more faith and more love, for example. Clarence Pickett, a colleague on the American Friends Service Committee, recalls that Jones' voice lifted in prayer would break through tense moments in sober discussions.

It is clear that prayer was a lifelong practice for Jones – we saw how as a child he experienced a type of prayer based on silence both informally with his family and more formally at Quaker meetings for worship. He admits that he found this quiet prayer and reflection hard to do on his own though: it was an art he had to learn, as he was by nature active and found it easier to be quiet in the company of others (he doesn't use the term extrovert, but he clearly was one). By his 40s, however, his previous habit of playing chess in the evenings had melted away, as he had learned the secret of withdrawal from the rush and turmoil of the world into the quiet cell of his inner self. 'It had become a joy to reflect, to meditate,' he said, 'to be a silent spectator of the drama going on behind the "footlights of consciousness".'[14] He emphasized that this tendency did not cut the nerve of action or make him smugly self-satisfied, however. On the contrary, living at a deeper level drove him all the more to share the tasks and problems of others.

In later years, Jones was happy to learn from practices in other religions. On one occasion when he was travelling with the Laymen's Foreign Missions Inquiry in the early 1930s, there was some consternation when a letter arrived from the National Christian Council of Japan complaining that commissioners were wasting too much time talking to Buddhists and Shintoists. The same day, an invitation arrived from a local Zen Buddhist monastery for an evening of Zazen meditation. Asked what they should do, Jones responded simply, 'We'll spend the evening with our Buddhist brethren.'[15] It was an experience that proved to be deeply moving. A few years later, in 1937, he wrote that Zen Buddhists had done more than most modern mystics to nurture inward calm. He warned, however, that meditation came with no guarantee that 'at the end of its long hard road there will be the desired meeting place – the Bethel of the soul'.[16]

Today there is a burgeoning research field into the mental, physical and emotional benefits of meditation, and how it leads to an increase in compassion. Jones would undoubtedly have been intrigued, as he felt religion should confer these benefits. I suspect, however, that he would have cautioned that an experience of God ran deeper than these neurological effects in the brain and physiological effects in the body.

Suggestions

What thoughts, feelings, images or memories come to mind when you think of prayer? Is there anything that attracts or disturbs you when reading about Jones' prayer life? Is prayer or meditation something you would like to explore further? If so, what initial step could you take?

A distinctively Quaker approach to gaining clarity through meditation can be found in Rex Ambler's *Light to Live By* and in the associated 'Experiment with Light' movement. More generally, there are any number of books on prayer from a Christian perspective. A classic that has some points of contact with Ambler's approach but has an Ignatian framework is *God of Surprises* by Gerard Hughes. Popular authors on meditation and the spiritual life from a Buddhist perspective include Thich Nhat Hanh and Matthieu Ricard.

5.3 Developing virtue

Learning how to sound the deeps of love, formation of purity, gentleness, tenderness of heart, freedom from harshness of judgment, absolute honesty of purpose and motive – these positive traits and qualities of life are far more important steps on the inner pathway than are artificial techniques of discipline.[17]

Jones learnt from his Uncle Eli that forming a good character required human effort, but we have also seen that he was convinced that this human effort was reinforced by divine help. From the above quotation, it is also the case that a good character leads us closer to God. It is a virtuous circle. An incident that brought this human–divine interaction home personally for Jones when he was a child occurred when he had done something he described as grieving his family (he doesn't provide any details). It was expected that Jones' mother would hand out a severe but rare punishment, but instead she took him to his room, knelt beside him, and prayed in a way that made Jones see 'just what I was, and no less clearly what I ought to be, and what with [God's] help I might be'.[18]

Jones doesn't give a definitive list of what he thought was involved in good character, but he says that from St Francis he learnt the infinite importance of gentleness, humility, simplicity and tenderness. A letter to his future wife, Elizabeth, however, revealed that he felt that an excess of humility could hold her back. What thee needs is 'courage and heart-boldness', he advises. Also, at various points in his books he extols 'spiritual fruit', which his readers would associate with Paul's list in Galatians 5: love, joy, peace, patience, kindness, goodness, faithfulness, gentleness and self-control.

One consequence of developing virtue is that a life that displays spiritual fruit is more likely to be an effective argument against materialism and secularism than clever arguments for the existence of God, Jones says, because wherever love is, there God is. Another is that it makes us happy! All Christ's beatitudes in the Sermon of the Mount attach to some inherent quality of life itself, he explains: the meek, the merciful and the pure in heart are happy not because the external world conforms to their wishes but because they have resources of life within themselves. Not only that, but this life can never be static, because 'the beatitude lies not in attainment, not in the arrival at a goal, but in the *way*, in the spirit, in the search, in the march'.[19] In other words, purity of heart, for example, has to do with the way one lives every day and there is always room for new depths to be plumbed. In practice, exercising and developing these virtues is likely to be tied up with service, which Jones felt was an invaluable help to the spiritual life.

Today, the 'positive psychology' movement associated with Martin Seligman has conducted much research into identifying and developing virtues, which are often discussed in terms of character 'signature strengths'. Briefly, a survey of the main religions revealed that they all endorse six virtues: wisdom and knowledge, courage, love and humility, justice, temperance, and spirituality and transcendence. As individuals, we naturally manifest some of these virtues more strongly than others, and it has been found that exercising and developing our own particular signature strengths makes us feel happier and more fulfilled. It is a finding that fits well with Jones' views.

Suggestions

What do you think your signature strengths might be? (There are various online tools to help you discover them if you are struggling, for example, at https://www.viacharacter.org/account/register.) Can you exercise and develop them more than you are doing at the moment?

Martin Seligman's book is *Authentic Happiness* (Nicholas Brealey, 2003).

5.4 Friendship

What counts most is the fellowship and influence of spiritually contagious persons who, beholding as in a mirror the glory of the Lord, unconsciously transmit that Life.[20]

Jones felt that it was essential that we should experience the fellowship and influence of 'spiritually contagious' people who know God. There is nothing else in this world that is richer and more wonderful than friendship, he enthused, and no way that is more effective at transmitting the spiritual fruit of life. When a life is set on fire and is radiant with self-consuming love, it will invariably set other lives on fire.

We saw in Chapter 1 how Jones was spiritually inspired at a young age by his Aunt Peace and Uncle Eli, and he considered himself fortunate to have been the giver and receiver of great friendships throughout his life. Many of these friendships helped him in his work. He recalls, for example, that the Philadelphia Quakers, in their loyal backing, were a tower of strength. Jones, in turn, passed on his vision and enthusiasm to others. Douglas Steere, for example, ended a letter to him by writing: 'Increasingly I appreciate how much these three years with you have meant to me and how good to me you have been at every turn. Know what a joy it is to be your associate.'[21]

It is his friendship with John Wilhelm Rowntree that stands out though. It was Rowntree, recall, to whom Jones had dedicated *Social Law* ('Dear friend over the sea with whom I have had a new revelation of the riches of human fellowship and the still deeper joy of fellowship with our Divine Companion'[22]). Rowntree had come to prominence as a young leader in the liberal reforms of British Quakerism, and it was he who had set Jones on this trajectory in America. He was ill with a rare kidney disease when Jones met him, and it was already causing him to lose his sight. He was known for facing his illness with a gentle and resolute courage, but would die at the age of 36. Intelligent, driven, personable, well-connected, and with a passionate vision for an educated, modern Quakerism, Rowntree was an ideal reforming partner. As Jones' biographer puts it, 'Their imaginations kindled each other; their enthusiasms matched. They gave each other strength.'[23]

In the light of the detrimental mental health effects caused by the isolation imposed during the COVID-19 pandemic, not many of us need scientific proof of the importance of friendship, although the proof is certainly there. Individuals vary in the number and depths of friendships they need or want to sustain, but humans are social animals, and those with a strong social network tend to be healthier both physically and emotionally. Spiritual friendship, of the type extolled by Jones, is often seen as adding an extra layer to friendship. In Celtic Christianity it is sometimes spoken of in terms of a soul friend, or *anam cara*, and in the Ignatian tradition it is sometimes formalized as 'spiritual direction' (although the term 'direction' is unfortunate, as the practice involves one person helping another to see where God might be acting in their lives, rather than telling them what to do). Whether they are formal or informal, however, spiritual friendships can enrich the spiritual journey immeasurably.

Suggestions

Jones said there was no technique by which one can contrive and achieve friendships – they just come. Most of us, however, find that they require effort, at least insofar as they need us to devote time to them. Is there anyone who inspires you spiritually that you would like to see more of? Is there anyone to whom you could offer spiritual inspiration or guidance? Spiritual direction in the Christian tradition is often available through local groups practising Ignatian spirituality, and it should be possible to find these online.

A sobering book considering the importance of friendship more generally, from the perspective of its increasing absence, is *The Lonely Century* by Noreena Hertz (Sceptre, 2020).

5.5 Study

It is manifestly impossible to crowd our religious dogmas and our sacred traditions into some compartment impervious to thought or to have them unaffected by the present day studies ... The cure for scepticism is always deeper knowledge.[24]

Jones was convinced that one of the reasons people stopped going to church was because what they heard was at variance with what they knew. And as we saw in the first half of this book, he endeavoured to mitigate this discrepancy by throwing himself whole-heartedly into studying new developments in psychology and philosophy and reformulating religious concepts such as the Inner Light in terms of them.

Jones was, of course, helped immeasurably in this task by the fact that he was a college lecturer: he was paid to study. He also had strong connections with Woodbrooke Study Centre in Birmingham. Woodbrooke opened at the turn of the twentieth century, when George Cadbury offered his grand house as a centre for education where Quakers could study social and religious issues to equip them for service, and it is still being used for that purpose today. Jones was offered the position of principal in 1902, but regretfully declined after deciding he could do more good by staying in America. He subsequently taught at summer schools there and elsewhere, however, describing them as the threshing floors where the grains of truth get pounded out with the flail of lectures, debate and controversy. He was also involved in the establishment of Pendle Hill in Philadelphia, which had similar aims to Woodbrooke.

Books were invaluable for study in Jones' era. Good books should be read, re-read and annotated, he advised, because great literature, written by persons who have been there, is one of the most vital influences in the discovery of the way. Memorization is also important: Jones says he memorized poetry and long passages from the Bible, which no doubt provided an ever-accessible store of analogies, inspiration and wisdom.

In spite of the fact that study took up such a huge part of his life, Jones recognized that it had its limits. While he embraced the new critical approach to the Bible, he was also aware that it could prevent us from reading the gospels as inspired literature. We need to see Christ with eyes of love and wonder, he insisted, and substitute the exclamation point for the overused question mark. When it came to the resurrection, he felt that it was and should remain a mystery. It was clear that the disciples were convinced that the Person they loved and followed was alive again after his crucifixion, and a vital presence in their lives first visibly and then inwardly, but not much more could be said. Science, too, had its limits: 'We do not surrender love and sympathy, goodness and patience, because we cannot dig them up with a pick or find them under the microscope.'[25] In line with this, he was convinced that the intellectual approach to God was only one of many. God is too rich and inclusive to be found by a single strand of our complex nature, he said. Thus, while a credible faith is important, so too is vision, insight, correspondence, pre-perception, quest, adventure, moral values, and the conviction of personal discovery.[26]

Furthermore, he recognized that it can be difficult to maintain a vital faith when studying theology. Critical thinking is fundamental to academia, so cherished beliefs tend to be questioned, and the student of theology who is also a Christian can be left feeling naïve, or become so head-centred that a sense of joy and trust evaporates. Jones complained that what he missed most in present-day Christianity with its confusions and controversies was the spirit of gentleness, of simplicity, of tenderness and grace. Teachers can play a crucial role in addressing this though, he thought, and should guide the spiritual life of their students rather than merely imparting knowledge: 'It is the teacher who discovers the hidden self in us and who sets it free, with its inherent capacities thrown into play, that matters most to us as we look back over the receding years.'[27]

Suggestions

If you have studied theology, does Jones' description of the spiritual problems it can cause ring true? Today, we can learn not just through books but also through podcasts, online lectures (e.g., TED) and free courses (e.g., through the platform Coursera). What type of learning suits you best? Is there an area of theology or spirituality that you would like to know more about? Is there a way you could explore it for a set time every week, either on your own or with others?

5.6 The role of suffering

The very discovery of the nearness of God, of the sustaining power of His love, of the sufficiency of His grace, has come to men in all ages through pain, and suffering and loss. We always go for comfort to those who have passed through deeps of life.[28]

Jones was no stranger to suffering. On an emotional level, we saw in Chapter 1 that he endured a tragic series of bereavements in the years around 1900. He also had a litany of health problems, suffering from severe asthma, sore eyes, insomnia, rheumatism, back problems that made it difficult to stand, a 'defective' digestive system later associated with a collapsed intestine, and dental problems. (The latter were exacerbated by a bad dentist, and seemed to cause secondary ailments: 'Satan has often had to bear the blame for deeply hidden pains and mysterious assaults which should have been charged up to the account of a blundering dentist,' he once commented wryly.[29]) In 1915 he suffered from a period of exhaustion that was labelled a nervous breakdown. Violet Hodgkin, who herself had known a long illness, wrote to him of the strange experience of having to lie like a starfish, high and dry on a beach, cut off from the tide (Figure 5). 'Only those who have known the deadly weariness of the beach can quite understand the living joy of the ocean once they get back there,' she said encouragingly.

Jones perceived that this suffering enriched his life in some ways though. Of the long period when he was bedbound with an infected foot as a child (described in Chapter 1), he wrote that he had unknowingly entered a phase when the threshold between the seen and unseen had worn thin, and the eternal became almost as real as the here and now. In part, this 'thinness' was expressed in the love and tender care of his mother and the faith of his Aunt Peace. On a particularly traumatic day, when a piece of bone could be seen poking through the wound, it was Peace who assured him with radiance and conviction, he said, that he was merely passing through a dark tunnel and God would make his coming days the best. Regarding his later health problems, he said they did not hinder him unduly, and that in fact not to know 'the ministry of pain' would have resulted in a loss of capacity for genuine sympathy. We always go for comfort to those who have passed through the deeps of life, he observed. Of Lowell's death, while acknowledging that learning to live with this loss was the hardest lesson on earth, shortly after being bereaved he could write that, 'The greatest service of the loved object is that it trains and prepares us for wider, more universal love.'[31]

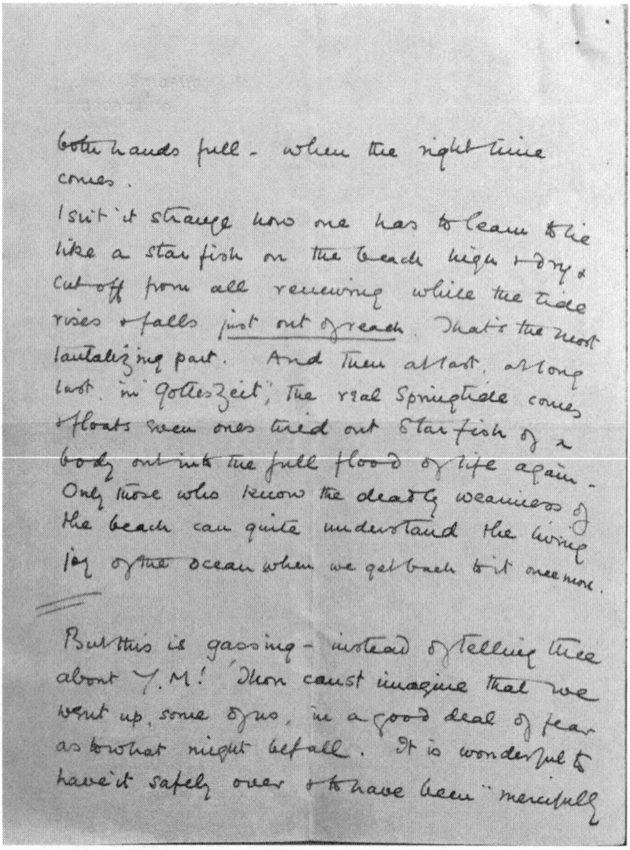
both hands full - when the right time
comes.
Isn't it strange how one has to learn to lie
like a star fish on the beach high & dry &
cut off from all renewing while the tide
rises & falls just out of reach. That's the most
tantalizing part. And then at last, at long
last, in "Gotteszeit", the real Springtide comes
& floats ones tired out Starfish of a
body out into the full flood of life again.
Only those who know the deadly weariness of
the beach can quite understand the living
joy of the ocean when we get back to it once more.

But this is gassing - instead of telling thee
about Y.M! Thou canst imagine that we
went up, some of us, in a good deal of fear
as to what might befall. It is wonderful to
have it safely over & to have been "mercifully

Figure 5: Extract of a letter from Violet Hodgkin in 1915, sympathizing with Jones' nervous exhaustion and drawing an analogy with a starfish.[30]

Jones was definitely not of the opinion that suffering should be sought though, and he denounced ascetic practices, which he thought produced abnormal persons, hysterical constitutions, and unnatural states such as trances. Even though he had personal experience that a life of joy and hope and service could be attained with impaired health, he viewed health as a blessing and a spring of optimism and joy. Health can be restored in various ways, he advised, both through medical intervention and through cultivating relaxation and serenity. Thus he actively sought out the best doctors for some ailments, for example, having an operation on his nose to ease his breathing, but found that fostering serenity worked mightily on nervous indigestion. For insomnia, he discovered that 'if one lies with muscles completely relaxed, with mind calm and serene, with spirit free from worry or fidgets and with life quietly committed to the Eternal Love that is underneath, the effect is just as restorative as sleep is'.[32] Likewise, sacrifice, surrender, and negation should not be actively sought or viewed as ends in themselves. Rather, they should be accepted as an inevitable part of a life that is rich and intense, because it is impossible to find without losing, to get without giving, or to live without dying.

Suggestions

Do you agree with Jones' view of suffering? What role has it played in your own life, or in the lives of those you know? If some suffering has led to spiritual growth and some has led to despair, can you discern anything that might have made the difference? Is there anything you can do to improve your own health, whether medically, by changing your lifestyle, or by cultivating serenity?

5.7 Appreciating beauty and nature

The appreciation of beauty, the enjoyment of 'whatsoever things are lovely,' is another agency of life which lies very close to religion and it is beyond question one of the great exalting and liberating influences. It both enlarges and consecrates man's life.[33]

Jones appreciated the beauty of the natural world right from childhood, as we saw in Chapter 1. The lake in front of the house was the first object of beauty that moved him. It gave him 'a primal pull upward', as at sunset he watched 'the extraordinary sheen flash across the water as the sun wrapped itself with multicoloured clouds in the far west'.[34] Later, he identified this pathway to God with the life of St Francis, who recognized that it was in the simple contacts with flowers and birds and little children that the glory of God and His eternal love are revealed to us. He also says that he had an appreciation of human character, recognizing early in life the difference between a pure and beautiful life and a showy but hollow one. An appreciation of beauty, or, put another way, the enjoyment of 'whatsoever things are lovely', enlarges and consecrates a person's life, he thought. He found confirmation of this in the fact that 'modern' educators had discovered that a love of beauty was a great ally to forming a fine character: a child that has a passion for beauty is morally safer than a child that has had this side of their character starved.

Jones saw beauty as eternal. Yes, appreciation of beauty has a subjective component, but it also puts us in touch with an overarching reality that is beyond us but not alien to our finite minds, he said. He describes going to the Louvre shortly after he graduated and seeing the Venus de Milo. To his surprise, he found his whole body quivering with emotion and knew that he was beholding not just a piece of marble but eternal beauty. That said, one shouldn't make beauty an end in itself and treat it as though it needed no Beyond to explain it, he cautioned. Beauty does not necessarily carry its devotees all the way home to the fatherland of the soul.

Jones found solace not only in the beauty of nature but also in hard physical exercise outdoors. Following his nervous breakdown in 1915, he took a holiday in Southwest Harbor on Mt Deste Island off the coast of Maine, and a chance encounter with a trail-maker saw him recover his strength by chopping trees and restoring paths. He also had a memorable trip to the Canadian Rockies in 1912 with two English friends, the Quakers Arnold Rowntree and Sir George Newman. Jones later wrote that they had lived thrillingly and dangerously on the trip and had come back with the great Northwest built into their imaginations and some of its rugged strength in their fibre. More generally, he found that fellowship, fresh air and beauty made walking holidays forever memorable.

There is increasing scientific support for the importance of contact with nature: its lack now even has a recognized name – nature deficit disorder. Relaxing or exercising outdoors, gardening, or keeping houseplants has been shown to improve our sleep, mental and physical health, and even our gut biome. Jones would not, I think, have been surprised.

Suggestions

What importance do you give to beauty in your life? What happens if you try to notice at least one instance of beauty every day (clouds, flowers, works of art, the strengths of someone's character, or the light in their eyes)? Can you spend more time in a 'green space', or bring the outside in by looking after a plant, hanging a birdfeeder, or displaying stones or shells? How does this affect your emotional or spiritual well-being?

The importance of nature is explored in, for example, *Losing Eden: Why Our Minds Need the Wild*, by Lucy Jones (Penguin, 2020).

***

Our exploration of Jones' ideas about the presence of God has revealed how he strove to weave together his personal experience with ideas from philosophy and psychology within a Christian framework. We have also seen, I hope, that his practices for cultivating that presence make up a well-rounded programme that addresses the spiritual, moral, emotional, social and intellectual facets of human nature. Jones' views on the presence of God within, or the Inner Light, can certainly be criticized. But perhaps his conviction that science and religion can both reveal God can inspire us. And perhaps his spiritual practices can enrich our lives, no matter what our beliefs.

Notes

Preface

1   E. Vining, *Friend of Life: The Biography of Rufus Jones* (Forgotten Books, [1958] 2012), 138.
2   H. E. Fosdick (ed.), *Rufus Jones Speaks to Our Time* (MacMillan, 1961), xii.
3   The first four chapters of this book are based on my PhD research, published as: H. Holt, *Mysticism and the Inner Light in the Thought of Rufus Jones, Quaker* (Brill, 2022).

Chapter 1

1   Vining, *Friend of Life*, 17.
2   R. M. Jones, *A Small-Town Boy* (MacMillan, 1941), 32.
3   R. M. Jones, *Finding the Trail of Life* (George Allen & Unwin, 1926), 65.
4   Jones, *Small-Town Boy*, 64.
5   R. M. Jones, *The Trail of Life in the Middle Years* (MacMillan, 1934), 211.
6   R. M. Jones, *Social Law in the Spiritual World* (Headley Brothers, 1904), frontispiece.
7   From Jones to John Willem Rowntree, 29 July 1904, Haverford Box 48.
8   From Edward Grubb, 14 November 1904, Haverford Box 8.
9   Vining, *Friend of Life*, 291.
10 R. M. Jones, *The Trail of Life in College* (MacMillan, 1929), 160.

Chapter 2

1   R. M. Jones, *Lighted Lives: A sermon preached in Trinity Church, Boston, 11 December 1932*. Retrieved from http://www.qhpress.org/quakerpages/qhoa/rmjll.htm [Accessed 5 December 2017].

2   Jones, *Middle Years*, 64–65.

3   See, e.g., R. W. Emerson, *The Essential Writings of Ralph Waldo Emerson*, ed. by B. Atkinson (Modern Library, 2000).

4   Quoted in Vining, *Friend of Life*, 92–93.

5   R. M. Jones, *Selections from the Writings of Clement of Alexandria* (Headley Brothers, 1910), 14.

6   Jones, *Trail of Life in College*, 180.

7   Jones, *Middle Years*, 7–8.

8   W. James, *The Varieties of Religious Experience* (Penguin [1902] 1985), 512 (italics as in the original).

9   Jones, *Social Law*, 135.

10   J. Royce, *The World and the Individual*, Vol. 2 (MacMillan, 1901), 417.

Chapter 3

1   R. M. Jones, *The Church's Debt to Heretics* (James Clarke & Co., 1924), 85.

2   R. M. Jones, *Practical Christianity* (General Books, [1905] 2012), 38.

3   R. M. Jones, *The Double Search* (John C. Winston, 1906), 45–46.

4   Jones, *Middle Years*, 88.

5   Jones, *Social Law*, 121.

6   R. M. Jones, *New Studies in Mystical Religion* (MacMillan, 1927), 204.

7   Letter from Gandhi, 28 May 1926, Haverford Box 25.

8   Letter from Joan Fry, 13 February 1905, Haverford Box 9.

9   R. M. Jones, *Pathways to the Reality of God* (MacMillan, 1931), 209.

10   R. M. Jones, *A Call to What Is Vital* (MacMillan, 1960), 112.

11   R. M. Jones, *Testimony of the Soul* (MacMillan, 1937), 171.

Chapter 4

1   C. E. Wolters (ed.), *The Cloud of Unknowing and Other Works* (Penguin, 1978), 62.

2   R. M. Jones, *The Luminous Trail* (MacMillan, 1947), 153.

3   Quoted in Vining, *Friend of Life*, 257.

4   Letter from Evelyn Underhill, 9 January 1928, Haverford Box 27.

5   Vining, *Friend of Life*, 207.

6   Vining, *Friend of Life*, 251.

7   Jones, *Social Law*, 142.

8   Jones, *Testimony*, 122.

9   W. Littleboy, *The Appeal of Quakerism to the Non-Mystic* (Friends Home Committee, 1916), 17.

10 C. F. Davis, *The Evidential Force of Religious Experience* (Oxford Scholarship Online, 1999), 69.

11 Jones, *Social Law*, 154.

12 Jones, *Middle Years*, 239.

13 Jones, *Social Law*, 124.

14 R. M. Jones, 'Why I enroll with the mystics', in *Contemporary American Theology* (Vol. 1), ed. V. Ferm (Round Table Press, 1932), 209.

15 Jones, 'Why I enroll', 207.

16 Jones, 'Why I enroll', 207.

17 Jones, *Middle Years*, 194–195.

18 Jones, *Social Law*, 155.

19 R. M. Jones, *Spiritual Reformers in the 16th and 17th Centuries* (MacMillan, 1914), xxvii.

20 Jones, *The Inner Life* (General Books [1917] 2012), 22.

21 Jones, *Testimony*, 30.

22 R. M. Jones, *Spiritual Energies in Daily Life* (General Books, [1922] 2012), pp. 3–4.

Chapter 5

1   Jones, *Testimony*, p. 29.

2   R. M. Jones, *Pathways to the Reality of God* (MacMillan, 1931), 248.

3   Jones, *Inner Life*, 17.

4   Jones, *Pathways*, 249–250.

5   Jones, *Social Law*, 195.

6   Jones, *Social Law*, 199.

7   T. Kelly, *The Eternal Promise* (Friends United Press, 2006), 43ff.

8   Kelly, *The Eternal Promise*, 53.

9   James, *Varieties*, 380–381.

10   Jones, *Inner Life*, 18.

11   Jones, *Testimony*, 22.

12   Jones, *Inner Life*, 17.

13   Jones, *Life in College*, 14.

14   Jones, *Life in College*, 200.

15   Vining, *Friend of Life*, 232.

16   Jones, *Testimony*, 29.

17   Jones, *Testimony*, 29-30.

18   Jones, *Finding the Trail*, 110.

19   Jones, *Inner Life*, 4.

20   Jones, *Testimony*, 30.

21   From Douglas Steere, 1 July 1931, Haverford Box 31.

22   Jones, *Social Law*, frontispiece.

23   Vining, *Friend of Life*, 72.

24   Jones, *Social Law*, 14–15.

25   Jones, *Social Law*, 42–43.

26   Jones, *Pathways*, 8.

27   Jones, *Life in College*, 12.

28   Jones, *Inner Life*, 5.

29   Jones, *Middle Years*, 175.

30   From Violet Hodgkin, 31 May 1915, Haverford Box 14.

31   Jones, *Practical Christianity*, 36.

32   Jones, *Middle Years*, 178.

33   R. M. Jones, *Religion as Reality, Life and Power* (HardPress [1919]), 17.

34   Jones, *Finding the Trail*, 50.

Bibliography

Books about Jones include the following.

Hinshaw, D. *Rufus Jones, Master Quaker*. Books for Libraries Press, 1953.

Holt, H. *Mysticism and the Inner Light in the Thought of Rufus Jones, Quaker*. Brill, 2022.

Vining, E. G. *Friend of Life: The Biography of Rufus M. Jones*. Forgotten Books, [1958] 2012.

Walters, K., ed. *Rufus Jones Essential Writings*. Orbis, 2001.

Some of the books by Jones referred to in the text are listed below. Some are available in scanned and reprinted form, or through online sites such as archive.org or hathitrust.org

Jones, R. M. *Social Law in the Spiritual World*. Headley Brothers, 1904.

Jones, R. M. *Practical Christianity*. General Books, [1905] 2012.

Jones, R. M. *Studies in Mystical Religion*. MacMillan, 1909.

Jones, R. M. *Spiritual Reformers in the 16th and 17th Centuries*. MacMillan, 1914.

Jones, R. M. *The Inner Life*. MacMillan, 1917.

Jones, R. M. *Spiritual Energies in Daily Life*. General Books [1922] 2012.

Jones, R. M. *The Church's Debt to Heretics*. Wipf and Stock, 1924.

Jones, R. M. *The Fundamental Ends of Life*. MacMillan, 1925.

Jones, R. M. *Finding the Trail of Life*. George Allen & Unwin, 1926.

Jones, R. M. *New Studies in Mystical Religion*. MacMillan, 1927.

Jones, R. M. *The Trail of Life in College*. MacMillan, 1929.

Jones, R. M. *Pathways to the Reality of God*. MacMillan, 1931.

Jones, R. M. 'Why I enroll with the mystics', In *Contemporary American Theology*, Vol. 1, edited by V. Ferm, 191–215. Round Table Press, 1932.

Jones, R. M. *Lighted Lives* A sermon preached in Trinity Church, Boston, 11 December 1932. Retrieved from: http://www.qhpress.org/quakerpages/qhoa/rmjll.htm.

Jones, R. M. *A Preface to Christian Faith in a New Age*. MacMillan, 1932.

Jones, R. M. *The Trail of Life in the Middle Years*. MacMillan, 1934.

Jones, R. M. *The Testimony of the Soul*. MacMillan, 1937.

Jones, R. M. *A Small-Town Boy*. MacMillan, 1941.

Jones, R. M. *The Luminous Trail*. MacMillan, 1947.

Jones, R. M. *Thou Dost Open Up My Life*, edited by M. H. Jones, Pendle Hill Pamphlet 127. Pendle Hill Publications, 1963.

Other books mentioned are as follows.

Ambler, R. *Light to Live by.* Quaker Books, 2008.

Davis, C.F. *The Evidential Force of Religious Experience*. Oxford Scholarship Online, 1999.

Hertz, N. *The Lonely Century.* Sceptre, 2020.

Hughes, G. *God of Surprises*. Darton, Longman and Todd, 2008.

James, W. *The Variety of Religious Experience*. Penguin [1902] 1985.

Jones, L. *Losing Eden: Why Our Minds Need the Wild*. Penguin, 2020.

Kelly, T. *The Eternal Promise*. Friends United Press, 2006.

McGilchrist, I. *The Master and his Emissary*. Yale University Press, 2009.

McGilchrist, I. *The Matter with Things* (Vols 1 and 2). Perspectiva Press, 2021.

Seligman, M. *Authentic Happiness.* Nicholas Brealey, 2003.

Details of the unpublished letters from the Rufus Jones Special Collection at Haverford College are available at http://www. haverford.edu/library/special/aids/rufusjones/rmjones.xml.

From Edward Grubb, 14 November 1904, Haverford Box 8.

From Joan Fry, 13 February 1905, Haverford Box 9.

From Violet Hodgkin, 31 May 1915, Haverford Box 14.

From Gandhi, 28 May 1926, Haverford Box 25.

From Evelyn Underhill, 9 January 1928, Haverford Box 27.

From Douglas Steere, 1 July 1931, Haverford Box 31.

From Jones to John Wilhelm Rowntree, 29 July 1904, Haverford Box 48.

CHRISTIAN ALTERNATIVE
BOOKS

THE NEW OPEN SPACES

Throughout the two thousand years of Christian tradition
there have been, and still are, groups and individuals that
exist in the margins and upon the edge of faith. But in
Christianity's contrapuntal history it has often been these
outcasts and pioneers that have forged contemporary
orthodoxy out of former radicalism as belief evolves to engage
with and encompass the ever-changing social and scientific
realities. Real faith lies not in the comfortable certainties of
the Orthodox, but somewhere in a half-glimpsed hinterland
on the dirt track to Emmaus, where the Death of God meets
the Resurrection, where the supernatural Christ meets the
historical Jesus, and where the revolution liberates both the
oppressed and the oppressors.

Welcome to Christian Alternative... a space at the edge where
the light shines through.
If you have enjoyed this book, why not tell other readers by
posting a review on your preferred book site.

Christian Atheist
Belonging without Believing
Brian Mountford
Christian Atheists don't believe in God but miss him:
especially the transcendent beauty of his music, language,
ethics, and community.
Paperback: 978-1-84694-439-0 ebook: 978-1-84694-929-6

Compassion Or Apocalypse?
A Comprehensible Guide to the Thoughts of René Girard
James Warren
How René Girard changes the way we think about God and
the Bible, and its relevance for our apocalypse-threatened
world.
Paperback: 978-1-78279-073-0 ebook: 978-1-78279-072-3

Diary Of A Gay Priest
The Tightrope Walker
Rev. Dr. Malcolm Johnson
Full of anecdotes and amusing stories, but the Church is still a
dangerous place for a gay priest.
Paperback: 978-1-78279-002-0 ebook: 978-1-78099-999-9

Readers of ebooks can buy or view any of these bestsellers by
clicking on the live link in the title. Most titles are published
in paperback and as an ebook. Paperbacks are available in
traditional bookshops. Both print and ebook formats are
available online.

Find more titles and sign up to our readers' newsletter at
http://www.johnhuntpublishing.com/christianity Follow us on
Facebook at https://www.facebook.com/ChristianAlternative

Also in this series

Quaker Quicks - Practical Mystics
Quaker Faith in Action
Jennifer Kavanagh
ISBN: 978-1-78904-279-5

Quaker Quicks - Hearing the Light
The core of Quaker theology
Rhiannon Grant
ISBN: 978-1-78904-504-8

Quaker Quicks - In STEP with Quaker Testimony
Simplicity, Truth, Equality and Peace - inspired by
Margaret Fell's writings
Joanna Godfrey Wood
ISBN: 978-1-78904-577-2

Quaker Quicks - Telling the Truth About God
Quaker approaches to theology
Rhiannon Grant
ISBN: 978-1-78904-081-4

Quaker Quicks - Money and Soul
Quaker Faith and Practice and the Economy
Pamela Haines
ISBN: 978-1-78904-089-0

Quaker Quicks - Hope and Witness in Dangerous Times
Lessons from the Quakers On Blending Faith, Daily Life, and Activism
J. Brent Bill
ISBN: 978-1-78904-619-9

Quaker Quicks - In Search of Stillness
Using a simple meditation to find inner peace
Joanna Godfrey Wood
ISBN: 978-1-78904-707-3